Montgomery Schnauzer P.I.
&
The Case of the Stealthy Cat Burglar

by Timothy Forner

Montgomery Schnauzer P.I.
&
The Case of the Stealthy Cat Burglar

Copyright © 2018, Timothy Forner

All rights reserved. No part of this publication may be reproduced or transmitted by any means, electronic, mechanical, photocopying or otherwise, without the prior permission of the author.

First published in 2019 by Timothy Forner

ISBN: 978-1-9995611-2-3

This is a work of fiction. All characters, places, names and proper nouns are the imagination of the author. Any resemblance to any persons, human, canine or other, either living or having crossed over the rainbow bridge, is purely coincidental.

Thanks

The author wishes to thank the following people for their support and contributions:

Aurora, Yale, Danielle and at everyone at Same Page for their faith and persistence;

Alina for the beautiful artwork that brought Monty's world to life;

Mario for the superb book design;

Olivia for the vibrant cover;

Sheelagh for her eagle-eyes;

Julia and Nayala, my first real readers;

Dad and Linda, the test readers whose encouragement kept me working;

my sister, Mrs. V., for introducing Monty to her class;

my patient and loving wife, Jody.

For Spencer,

the most special dog any family could ask for

Chapter One

Starting Over

One cute little dog stared out of a kennel at the animal shelter. There were many dogs at the shelter (sadly), but he was a particular type of dog. He had dapper gray fur, styled with a handsome haircut. It was short on top and long on his belly and legs. He had a fluffy beard around his prominent snout, and a flourish of eyebrows over his soulful eyes. He was a gentleman in a dog's body. He was a Miniature Schnauzer.

This was something to be proud of, he was sure. His master had told him so. The man said he was special, and a special dog needed a special name. That's how he got his full name: Montgomery P. Schnauzer.

His master called him Monty, because his full name was too official for everyday use. He only used it when Monty was bad (rarely), or when the two of them worked on a case. That was what they were doing when Monty last saw his beloved master.

It was a few nights ago. Monty was sitting with his master, while the man read aloud from one of his detective books. His master knew a lot about detective work. The man had tons of books on the subject. He read to Monty almost every night.

They were reading a particularly good story that night. Then the man fell asleep, and he

Starting Over

did not wake up again. This frightened Monty. He barked and barked and barked until his throat was sore.

Finally, someone came to help. But they took his master away. They brought Monty here to the animal shelter and locked him in a kennel.

Now he was waiting, but he did not know for what. And he didn't know how that story ended. He was pretty sure the butler had something to do with it, but would he ever find out?

Poor Monty had never felt so afraid and so alone.

Montgomery Schnauzer P.I.

Starting Over

Monty had lost count of the days. How long had he been stuck here at the animal shelter? He wasn't sure. It was late afternoon, he judged by the fading light through the window, when two people came to visit the animal shelter. He heard the main door open down the hall and around the corner, and then he heard two women talking.

"I don't think this is a good idea," said the first woman. She had a sweet melodious voice.

"Hear me out," the second woman said. Her voice had a gravelly tone. "It's been months since Phil. You're by yourself all the time. It's not healthy, Sarah. I think a companion would be good for you."

"I'm just here to look so you'll stop bugging me. I've never had a pet. I wouldn't know what to do with one!"

"You can figure it out together. That's the point to getting a pet. Start with a cat. They're easier."

"I'm allergic to cats."

"OK. A dog it is. How about this one?"

"Too big. It would never fit in my apartment."

"Something smaller then. Here's a poofy white one. He's cute. What's his name?"

"The sign says Priscilla."

"Oh. She is cute. Could you see yourself with a Priscilla?"

Starting Over

"I can't see myself with a dog. I'm only here to look. Will you back off already?"

"Alright. I'm backing off. You look."

At last, the women came around the corner, and Monty could see them. The first woman was tall and blonde. Her perfume smelled like strawberries. Monty liked strawberries. His master used to feed them to him at breakfast. The other woman hung back, with her arms folded on her chest. The blonde woman came over to Monty's pen.

"Just looking," she said, softly. Monty noticed she was the one with the pleasing voice.

Monty knew all about looking. He decided to help. He looked directly at her. He fixed his big, brown puppy-dog eyes at her burning blue human eyes. He looked long and deep at those eyes. He strived to give his most thoughtful stare.

The next thing Monty knew, the blonde woman put him in her car.

She talked as she drove, "Well... my name is Sarah. The shelter said your name is Montgomery. But that's too long. I'm going to call you Monty."

"That would be fine," Monty said.

He talked without making noise. It's a matter of fact that dogs (and most animals) talk with body language and expressions. Humans can do it too, but most have forgotten how.

"I hope that's OK," she continued talking. "I can't believe I'm doing this. This is so unlike me. I don't know. I guess maybe Gail was right. Maybe I do need some company. You see, I've been on my own since... Wait a minute. Why am I talking to a dog?"

"Because," Monty said, with a silent twitch of his ears, "we are such good listeners."

Sarah kept silent for a while. But then she started talking again. She talked a lot about what the heck she was going to do now. Monty got the impression she thought he could not understand. He did, of course. Monty was proud of his knowledge of human words. That, he supposed, was the benefit of having a master who read to him every night — mystery novels mostly. They both loved a good mystery.

Montgomery Schnauzer P.I.

She talked.

And Monty listened.

Chapter Two

Strange New Home

The car arrived at a big tower that stretched toward the sky. It had windows and patios on every floor. The car rolled to a stop at a square cave, blocked by a wall that looked like a cage. Monty thought the drive was over, but to his surprise, the cage wall slid up. It was actually a door. They rolled through this doorway and into a big cavern filled with cars.

What was this place? Monty wondered. It looked like a kennel for cars. Do cars sometimes run away? Monty's master always left the car outside, and it never wandered off.

They drove down a slope, around a corner, and past rows of parked cars. They came to an empty spot. Sarah worked the steering wheel. The car slid in between two other cars and came to a stop in front of a concrete wall.

Sarah got out, walked to the other side, and opened Monty's door. She lifted him out of the car and put him on the hard concrete floor.

"Come on," Sarah said, and she started walking away.

Monty froze. Sarah's voice echoed in the huge and hollow space. Every step she took sounded like thunder. How scary! But the smell was even worse. The place stunk of cars. Monty's sensitive nose could smell lots and lots of cars, and aside from Sarah's wonderful perfume, not much else. This place gave him a serious case of the heebie-jeebies.

"Monty, come," Sarah said.

"I can't," Monty said. "I'm scared."

"Oh for Pete's sake, it's just a parking garage!"

"A park and what?"

"Come on!"

Monty gathered his courage and trotted after her. He certainly did not want to get left here. This was a *park-in-a-garage* all right, he thought. It had to be the worst park ever! There were no trees, no grass, no plants at all. It wasn't even open to the sky. Only a stupid car could mistake this place for a park!

They came to a weird shiny door. It made a humming noise. Then it slid open to the side to reveal a tiny square room with no exit. It didn't lead anywhere at all.

"Get in the elevator," Sarah said, coaxing him to enter.

That was another new word for Monty. The place looked like a closet. Why didn't she call it a closet? He soon learned that *elevator* meant *magic room*. They got in at the park-in-garage. The doors closed. And when they opened again, Monty and Sarah were in a totally different place. They stepped into a hallway with lots more doors. These were the standard type, with doorknobs and locks like you would find on the front of a house. Sarah stopped in front of one.

"This is it." she said. "Home sweet home."

Strange New Home

How could she tell? It must be the smell, Monty thought. He gave it a sniff. It smelled a little like her, along with a few other scents he could not place. He took another big, long sniff in order to remember it.

That hall door turned out to be the front door to Sarah's small house. Curious, Monty felt the need to investigate. As a dog, his nose was far more sensitive than his eyes or even his ears. Countless new smells waited for him in Sarah's home. He wanted to observe and record every detail of every room.

He started with the kitchen. Like most dogs, Monty loved food, and so starting with the food smells made sense. Alas, he found the kitchen disappointing. There weren't many food scents, and most of them lingered around the microwave. He smelled a lot of tea, but boiled leaves did not interest him. Monty concluded that Sarah did not cook very much.

He moved into the next room. By the look of the furniture it was a living and dining area. He could smell Sarah's scent most strongly around the couch. There were food smells there too, between the couch and the coffee table. Monty concluded that Sarah dined while watching TV.

Monty passed another bigger door, like the kind that usually open to the outside. It was closed. He made a mental note to come back to it later. He padded down a hallway and came to a bathroom on his left, a place of many strong smells. This was clearly the source of Sarah's sweet smelling perfume, but there were many other scents: minty toothpaste, hair products, water, and at least three different kinds of soap (yuck!). These were strongest in the bathtub. Conclusion: Sarah took a lot of baths. The human fascination with baths baffled Monty. Dogs, as a rule, detested them.

Monty moved from the bathroom to the bedroom. Both rooms held the distinct smell of Sarah. But in the bedroom, he picked up the faint trace of another person's scent. It wasn't in the sheets or pillows, more likely in the mattress. And it was old. Conclusion: whoever left this smell behind hadn't been here for quite a while.

"Phew," he heard Sarah say from the other room. "Time to open this door and cool the place off."

Montgomery Schnauzer P.I.

Strange New Home

He heard a door open, and felt a whoosh of fresh air. That must be the back door.

"Outside!" Monty barked. He rushed over, eager to check out the back yard.

"Wow, that got your attention," Sarah said.

Monty skipped out to the patio. He wanted to run into the yard like he used to do at his own home. But he stopped cold. There was no back yard. There was only sky. Monty looked around, trying to make sense of it. Where was the ground? He walked to the edge. He spied the ground far, far below. Sarah's house, it seemed, hung impossibly high in the sky. Oh no, this would not do! Monty did not want this to be his home. He wanted his real home, back with his beloved master.

Monty wondered how long he was expected to stay here. He spent the rest of the day with this woman he had only just met. That night, he learned the place did have one nice thing. Sarah invited him up on the human bed. He had never been on a human bed before. He really wanted to try it. He jumped up. Oh my, he thought, how wonderful! It had just the right feel to it: not too soft, not too firm. Monty curled up on it, only for minute, to test it out. It was so comfortable! He drifted off to sleep. And he dreamed of the great detective Sherlock Holmes.

Strange New Home

Montgomery Schnauzer P.I. ———————

Chapter Three

City Life

Monty awoke to find he'd slept all night. The morning sun flooded the room. His new friend, Sarah, busied herself in the kitchen. He smelled eggs and fried potatoes. Yum! Now, the new house had two things he liked: the big, soft bed and breakfast!

Monty savored every bite. Sarah's cooking tasted so much better than the kibble at the animal shelter.

As soon as he finished eating, she whisked him out to the magic elevator room. This time it took them to a large open room with high ceilings and a polished tile floor. Monty followed Sarah through a pair of glass doors. Then they stood outside in the sunny spring afternoon, in a strange neighborhood.

More towers like the one Sarah lived in lined the street. Cars buzzed up and down the road like giant bugs. Sarah and Monty walked along the sidewalk. This neighborhood seemed alive, filled with much more activity than his previous home in the sleepy suburbs. He saw people here and there. He heard noises all around him. He smelled new scents everywhere. Oh the smells! He wondered if he could absorb them all. Monty felt overwhelmed.

He sniffed along the edge of the sidewalk. Then he noticed he was missing the scents

City Life

on the other edge of the sidewalk. He crossed over to smell them. Now he missed the smells along the first edge. He had to cross back again – and so on, and so on.

He smelled scents left by many other dogs. He'd never met any of them, so the scents meant nothing to him. He sniffed the legs of the people they passed. He didn't know any of them either. He worried how he would ever fit in to this new place?

They stopped at a store with tables and chairs outside. He smelled a familiar scent: coffee. It instantly reminded Monty of his master. The man used to drink a lot of coffee. Monty felt sad. He also felt bad that he enjoyed Sarah's house so much that he forgot about his master for a while. He vowed not to let that happen again.

Sarah opened the door to the coffee shop. Monty tried to step inside. Sarah tugged on the leash and stopped him short.

"No dogs allowed," she said.

What? Why? Monty did not understand.

She wrapped his leash around a chair leg. Then she went inside. The door closed in his face.

Monty looked around the little patio area. He saw two small dogs tied to a table. They looked exactly the same. How odd! Both of them had light brown fur with black around the muzzle. They each had the same floppy ears, big eyes and pushed-in noses. Monty moved beside one dog and looked at the other. He expected to see a mirror with another Monty in it. But no. That meant both dogs had to be real. Monty sniffed each dog carefully. His nose told him things that his eyes did not. They both smelled similar, but there were differences, too. These dogs were twins.

The twins looked at each other as if they shared the same thought. At exactly the same time they both said, "What are you looking at, fuzz face?!"

Monty jumped back in surprise. The twins laughed.

One of them said, "Got ya, didn't we?"

The other said, to no one in particular, "Ha ha! That was a good one!"

Montgomery Schnauzer P.I.

Monty stared at the rude little dogs.

"Oh, we're sorry, stranger. My name is Licky."

"And I'm Sticky."

Monty now felt like he was being rude. He should introduce himself. "I am Montgomery P. Schnauzer," he said.

The twins blinked.

Monty felt awkward in the silence, like something was missing. He added, "Son of a famous detective."

Just then, another dog walked up. His human wrapped the leash around a chair leg, and went inside. The new dog was light brown, tall and lean, and a little bit twitchy. One of his ears stood up, and one flopped over. He nodded a greeting at the twins and Monty.

Licky (or was it Sticky?) introduced the new dog, "This is Jiff."

The other twin whispered in Monty's ear, "He's not quite right, you know... up here." Sticky (or was it Licky?) put his paw to his head.

Jiff did not hear, or perhaps he didn't mind. He said, "Hi, my name is Jiff."

Licky (perhaps Sticky) said, "This is Mont... uh... something. He's a detective."

"Actually," Monty said, "I'm the son of –"

A hollow booming sound interrupted Monty, drowning out his words. It sounded a bit like a bark, and yet not like any bark he'd ever heard. A big black vehicle (an S.U.V.) pulled up and parked on the other side of the street.

City Life

The noise came from inside it, echoing with a frightening tone.

Jiff's eyes opened wide. He shivered uncontrollably. The twin dogs' big, bulgy eyes grew even bigger. Monty was not one to spook at odd sounds. But clearly this sound frightened the other dogs, and that unnerved him. What did they know that he didn't?

"Stay away from that car, if you know what's good for you," said Licky (or so Monty presumed; he'd given up trying to guess which twin was which).

"Yeah," Sticky agreed. "That's a monster."

Monty looked the vehicle over. Instead of back windows, it had metal grates. No one could see what was inside. Two police officers got out of the front. They walked past the dogs and into the coffee shop. Monty looked at the police officers, then at the vehicle, and then back at the know-it-all twins.

"You can't be serious," Monty said.

Across the street, two children skipped past the black car. This sparked a new and angrier snarling fit from inside.

"Told you," Licky said.

Sticky nodded, "Monster."

Jiff wiggled himself under the table. He trembled with fear so badly he rattled the whole table.

Finally, Sarah came out, carrying a huge cup. Monty smelled coffee and soy and sugar-free vanilla. She took Monty away from his new friends. He looked back. Jiff was still hiding under (and vibrating) the table. Licky and Sticky cast Monty decided looks.

"You know we're right about the monster," one twin said.

His brother nodded.

Montgomery Schnauzer P.I. ⸻

Chapter Four
A Park for Dogs

Sarah led Monty away from the coffee shop, down a different sidewalk. It curved around the other side of the tall buildings, away from the busy road. Monty felt relieved to get away from the whooshing cars. He did not like them whipping by while he tried to enjoy a nice walk. Why weren't all sidewalks like this?

And he enjoyed this walk very much! The sun shone high in the sky. A gentle breeze freshened the air. The birds in the trees sang a cheery bird song:

It's a happy day!

In the beautiful world!

What a glorious day,

To be... a bird!

Monty agreed. The day did indeed look beautiful. However, the silly birds were missing all the smells! On his left side, the townhouses had narrow little gardens. He could smell the flowers. He could smell the marking spots left behind by other dogs. He could even smell the mice that hid in their nests, deep inside the safety of the plants. On Monty's right, he could smell water and salt.

That must be the ocean! Monty thought. He pulled at his leash, almost dragging Sarah with him, to get to the edge of the sidewalk and take in the wonder of the ocean.

Sarah was already fed up with Monty's zigzagging when he suddenly pulled hard to the right. He crossed in front of a man walking and fiddling with his phone. The man wasn't paying attention, and the leash made a perfect tripwire. Sarah sprang forward with her hand out.

"Excuse me! Wait!" she said.

The man jumped back, startled. But at least he didn't trip over the leash.

"I'm sorry," Sarah said. "He's new. This is our first —"

The man scowled and stomped off, his attention focused again on his phone.

Sarah paused to catch her breath. So far, this dog walk had been super frustrating for her. If her new pet wasn't pulling, he was lagging behind, and that wasn't the first stranger they almost tripped. Now Monty sat simply staring out at the water. What the blazes was he looking at?

She had to admit the water looked pretty. She stood for a moment, taking in the view. A calmness settled over her. She'd lived here for years, but now she felt as if she were seeing the ocean for the first time.

When she felt they'd paused long enough, she said, "Come on, you silly dog. Don't you want to get to the park?"

A Park for Dogs

Monty looked up at Sarah, "Did you say park?"

Sarah tugged on the leash, and Monty followed. He thought, a park! It had been so long since he had been to a park. The sidewalk branched. The left path rounded back between the buildings, while the right path followed the shoreline. They followed the shoreline path, and it led them right into a park.

Monty's nose went into overdrive. Every dog knows that park smells are the best smells.

They passed a playground full of happy children and watchful parents. They walked through a small grove of trees. They came to a field of grass. There, Monty saw an amazing sight.

The field teemed with bounding, playing dogs. Monty had never seen so many dogs in one place. And to his surprise, they were all off-leash! Sarah reached down and removed Monty's leash. He looked up at her in disbelief. This was too good to be true! Yet Monty stood where he was. There were so many dogs, and he didn't know anybody. He suddenly felt unsure of himself.

Pretty soon, a familiar face showed up – twice. Licky and Sticky bounded up to greet Monty.

"Oh look," said Licky (or Sticky), "it's Mont, ah... Mount, uh... Milt? um..."

"I think it's Montage," said Sticky (or Licky).

"Hi Montage!" said both.

"You guys can call me Monty."

"Oh good. That's easier."

"Come on, Monty. We'll show you around. I've always said, you can't sniff out new friends just sitting on your butt!"

"So true, Stickster." said Licky.

Monty made a mental note that this twin was definitely Licky, which would make the other one Sticky.

The two little dogs moved around the park with confidence. They seemed to know everyone. They ran from dog to dog, with Monty following. Each time they stopped for a brief chat, they introduced him as "the great detective Monty." Monty tried to explain that

A Park for Dogs

he was only the son of a great detective. None of the other dogs understood. It occurred to Monty that maybe they didn't know what a detective was.

But one dog did.

A girl dog strode over. She had a stocky build and a pushed-in face, similar to the twins. But she was a larger dog, and she had a coat of tan and white, like a caramel sundae. She ignored Licky and Sticky as if they weren't there at all. She went right up to Monty.

"So. You're a detective?" she said.

She smelled beautiful — a mix of girl dog, slobber, and the dirt she'd just rolled in. For a second, Monty had trouble finding his voice.

"The son of a detective," he said. "My name is Monty."

"Well, I'm Duchess, and I have a problem." She sounded impatient.

Monty recognized her type from the stories his master used to tell him. She was a classic "dame in distress". Usually, the gumshoe (that's book talk for private detective) was well advised to avoid this person. Unfortunately for the hero, there's often a catch.

"I buried a bone in this park, and now I can't find it. Someone stole it!"

And when Monty did not respond, she said, "I need your help."

There was the catch. This dame had a case. No detective could resist a new and interesting case. Every mystery fan knew that. What would Monty's beloved master have him do? Monty was pretty sure the man would want him to help. The words came out of his mouth so fast, Monty was not sure he'd said them.

"I will take your case, madam."

Montgomery Schnauzer P.I. ───────────────

Chapter Five

Unearthing a Mystery

Monty wondered what he had got himself into. He wasn't a detective. His master was the detective. Monty always fancied he would make a great detective one day. He supposed today was as good as any to start. And there's no better place to start a new case than at the scene of the crime.

He told his new client to bring him to where she last saw her bone. Duchess took him to the far edge of the park. They were near the buildings again. She gestured to the corner of the last building.

"I live right over there," she said. "We had a barbecue two nights ago. Oh, I just love barbecues! Don't you?"

Monty had never had a barbecue, so he couldn't comment on the topic. No matter, as she didn't wait for an answer.

"Well, I had a nice big steak bone left over. It had hours of chewing left on it. I didn't want it to go to waste, so I buried it..."

She ducked into the bushes, out of sight from the rest of the park. She stopped at a little pile of loose dirt next to a dog-dug hole.

And then she finished her sentence, "Right here."

Unearthing a Mystery

Monty put his nose to the ground and went to work. He sniffed the area thoroughly. The steak-bone smell was present, but it was faint. Maybe she didn't dig deep enough. He put his paws in the hole and dug – and dug and dug and dug. His nose told him he'd dug past the point where the bone had been. That proved it: the bone was truly missing. But wait, there was something else there. He dug a little more and turned up a velvet bag. He grabbed it in his teeth and shook the dirt off it. It had rocks in it.

"What the bark?!" Duchess said. "Who would bury a bag of rocks?"

Monty plopped the little bag on the loose dirt in front of him.

"That's a good question," he said. "If we find who left these rocks, we'll find who took your bone." He hoped he sounded like Humphrey Bogart playing Sam Spade in *The Maltese Falcon*.

"Terrific!" Duchess replied. "How do we do that?"

"By smell, of course. With the scent of this bag, we can track the thief."

Sarah's mood had improved. She actually enjoyed herself at the dog park. She even met a new friend, Wendy, who had a *rescue dog* named Jiff. Rescue dog was a term Wendy used to describe an orphaned dog that got adopted into a new family. Sarah supposed Monty was a rescue dog too.

Poor Jiff had been adopted once before, but that family could not handle his special needs. Wendy had a lot of experience with dogs, and she volunteered to take Jiff and help him with his issues. Wendy explained that Jiff had come a long way since she adopted him. Wendy also gave first-timer Sarah some advice on how to handle her new dog.

"You're a family now," she said, "you and Monty."

"Don't you mean a pack, like a group of wolves?" Sarah asked.

"Not exactly. Dogs aren't wolves. They're domestic pets. You make the rules and enforce them. If you don't, Monty will run wild. But you can't enforce them like some tyrant. Think of yourself more like his mother."

Sarah laughed out loud. The thought of a person being a mother to a dog was ridiculous.

"I'm serious," Wendy said. "Watch this."

Wendy turned to her dog and said, "Jiff, who's your momma? Who's your momma!"

Jiff came closer to Wendy. He leaned his shoulder against her legs and raised his head up. Wendy patted him down. He seemed to love it. He rolled his head from side to side with his mouth open and his tongue hanging out. Wendy stopped.

She said, "Sit, Jiff."

Jiff sat. And he gazed at her with his big, brown eyes.

"See?" Wendy said to Sarah. "He knows I'm in charge, but he also knows that I love him.

It's the energy I give out that he responds to. Try it with Monty. Uh, where did he go?"

The last Sarah saw of Monty, he was playing in the bushes.

She called for him, "MONTEEEE!"

Monty did not come.

"He doesn't know your voice yet," Wendy said. "You'd better go get him."

Sarah set off to collect her dog.

She found Monty in the far corner of the park, along with a British Bulldog. The two dogs had dug a huge hole, like they were trying to find the center of the Earth.

"Gah! What are you doing?" Sarah exclaimed.

Montgomery Schnauzer P.I.

She caught herself. Wendy told her to treat Monty like a child. She took a deep breath to calm down. When she spoke again, she tried to sound like a mother. And she felt foolish.

"Monty," she said, "that's not appropriate behavior."

Monty didn't recognize Sarah's voice at first. He had only been with her for a day. Her voice wasn't exactly burned in his brain.

"Monty, pay attention!" Sarah said, "It's time to go."

Was it Monty's imagination, or did she sound like a TV show mom?

Montgomery Schnauzer P.I.

Sarah stomped over to him. Instinctively, Monty put his paw on the bag of rocks to hide it from her. He had no reason to believe she would interfere, but he barely knew her and she seemed angry. He thought it best to leave Sarah out of his detective business.

Monty addressed his client, "Duchess, I have to go, but we'll pick this up tomorrow. OK?"

"Oh, but why can't we do it now? I want to get that son-of-a-cat!"

Duchess was impatient and frustrated. Monty understood that. But catching the thief would be easier said than done. They could track him, sure. But who knew where the trail would lead? It probably went to some *smoky gin joint* — whatever that was. Monty did not know, but it showed up time and again in detective stories.

He was also beginning to think his new lady friend had a bit of a potty mouth.

Monty tried to explain, "Investigations take time. There's a process."

But that's all he got out. Sarah interrupted and clipped the leash on him.

"We're going," Sarah said, and she turned and marched off.

Monty barely had time to scoop up the bag of rocks before the leash yanked on his collar.

"Tomorrow," he assured Duchess. Then he left with the bag of rocks swinging from his mouth.

Montgomery Schnauzer P.I. ─────────────

Chapter Six

Complications with the Law

Sarah kept her back to Monty as she led him out of the bushes. He followed dutifully, trying not to draw attention to himself. He worried – what would she do when she saw the bag of rocks? Would she try to take them away? They stepped out from behind the bushes. He was in the open now. It would be harder to keep his secret – impossible, actually. She would see them eventually.

Montgomery Schnauzer P.I.

The simple dog from the coffee shop was there with a woman.

"Hi, my name is Jiff," said the dog.

Monty replied, "Yes, we already did this. I'm Monty."

Wendy spoke to Sarah, "We'll walk with you. Monty might learn a thing or two from Jiff."

"Hey!" Monty said, offended. He wondered what this woman thought he needed to learn, and he seriously doubted he could pick much up from Jiff. But walking together gave him an idea. Monty moved to the opposite side of Jiff, away from Sarah.

He said, "Jiff, stay close to me. I need to hide behind you."

"Uh, sure," Jiff said.

Complications with the Law

They all walked as a group, and Monty stayed out of Sarah's view behind Jiff. Sarah didn't notice his bag of rocks. She chatted with her new friend. Monty listened to their conversation and learned the woman's name was Wendy.

They strolled as far as Wendy's building. Then the two women said goodbye. Wendy walked away with Jiff, and Monty lost his cover. Sarah noticed he had something in his mouth.

"Hey, what have you got?" she said.

Monty turned his head away. The bag swung from his mouth.

"That does not look like an appropriate dog toy," Sarah said.

"It's not a toy. It's evidence," Monty said.

"Come on. Give me that," Sarah said, and she reached out to him.

"Nooo!" Monty growled at her.

She jumped back in shock, not expecting that kind of resistance. She reached out again, swiftly this time, and caught hold of the bag.

"No, I need those!" Monty protested. He clenched his jaws and tugged hard. Sarah stumbled forward. Her grip went slack. For a second, he thought he'd won, but she regained her balance.

"What's the matter with you?" Sarah said. "You let go! Right now!"

They were locked in a tug-of-war. Sarah was much bigger, but Monty was determined. He

Complications with the Law

hung on tight. She pulled so hard she dragged him forward, but still he held on to his prize.

"Bad dog!" Sarah scolded.

Monty let go. She fell back on her butt.

Her words struck him numb: bad dog. Was he really? How could that be? If there was one thing Monty knew for sure about himself, it was that he was a good dog. His master had always told him so. Now he was... he was a... Monty couldn't even think the words. He hung his head in shame.

Sarah got back on her feet. She turned the small bag over in her hands. She brushed the dirt off it. Then she pulled open the draw string and looked inside.

Montgomery Schnauzer P.I.

Complications with the Law

Monty pleaded with his soulful stare, "I need those back. They're the only clue for my first case."

Sarah looked up. For half a second, Monty let himself hope she understood him. But she didn't even look at him. She stared into space with a shocked expression. Then she looked in the bag again. She put her finger inside and stirred the little stones.

At last she said, "Come on, Monty. We need to go for a ride."

She tugged on his leash and guided him the rest of the way home. Instead of going upstairs, the magic elevator room took them to the park-in-garage. He gave up protesting. She clearly did not understand a word he said.

Complications with the Law

She walked him to the car and put him in the passenger seat.

Monty tried to think. Why would finding a bag of rocks prompt an immediate car ride? Nothing came to mind. He decided to pay close attention to the route. While Sarah drove, Monty hung his head out the window.

Not long after, the car stopped. Sarah got out. She lifted Monty out and then led him by his leash. They went into a building. The reception area was small and plain and furnished with only a few chairs. Monty tried to sniff around, but the leash only let him go so far. Sarah went to the front counter, where a man stood behind a thick sheet of glass. She leaned close to the glass and tried to talk through it. That muffled her voice, and Monty couldn't hear what she said. The man disappeared into the back. Sarah turned around and sat in one of the chairs.

"Come, Monty," she said. "Sit."

Monty glared at her. What was her problem? He was on a case, and she took his only clue. She brought him to this weird place. And now she just wanted to sit around?!

"Monty!" Sarah said. "For heaven's sake, we're at the police station!"

Oh, so this was what a police station looked like! Monty was surprised. The detective stories talked about them. But this was quite different from what he had pictured in his mind.

A side door opened, and a different man walked in. He wore a police uniform. He walked up to Sarah to talk to her. He talked fast and

Complications with the Law

used some big words Monty didn't know. Monty came in close to pick up as much as he could.

"I understand you have something to turn in," the policeman said.

Sarah said, "Yes, I found... uh... my dog, actually, found... these." She presented the bag of stones.

The policeman had a plastic bag. He held it open in front of him. Sarah got some meaning from that. She dropped Monty's evidence into the plastic bag.

"Wait," Monty said. "What are you doing?"

"I think they're diamonds," Sarah said to the policeman.

"They're mine, is what they are!" Monty said. "And I still need them."

"Thank you for bringing them in. You've done the right thing," the policeman said to Sarah.

No one paid any attention to Monty. His frustration mounted. He kept his eyes on the plastic bag with the velvet pouch inside.

"I can't tell you much, ma'am. There is a cat burglar operating in the city," the policeman explained.

Monty's ears perked up at the mention of a cat. He knew for a fact that cats could not be trusted. He would bet his reputation that this cat had something to do with the bone theft. Admittedly, he didn't have much of a reputation, but that would change for the better if he could catch that cat burglar.

Complications with the Law

The policeman continued, "This could be his work. I can't tell you more. This is an ongoing investigation."

"Of course, I understand," Sarah said. She stood up and extended her hand.

Monty thought, with relief, that she was reaching to get the rocks back. Instead, she shook the policeman's hand. Monty knew this as human body language for goodbye.

He barked, "Hey! Don't forget my clues! The rocks! The diamo-thingies! Get them!"

"Monty! Hush!" Sarah ordered.

"No! I need those! Give them back!"

Monty lunged at the plastic bag. He didn't realize that the humans only heard, "Bark!

Bark bark bark! Bark bark bark!" And to them, he appeared to be attacking the police officer.

"No! Monty! Down!" Sarah wailed. She pulled on his leash, tugging him backwards. Monty flailed his front paws in the air, as his rear paws slid on the floor.

"I'm sorry," Sarah said to the policeman.

"It's OK. He doesn't look dangerous," the policeman laughed. "Have a nice day. And keep your doors locked." He turned and walked away. Sarah dragged Monty toward the outside door.

Monty shouted, "Not dangerous?! I'll show you. Give me back my rocks or I'll –"

Monty found himself outside. There wasn't much point in finishing that sentence. The door to the police station closed in his face.

Complications with the Law

Sarah led Monty to the car. She put him in the passenger seat, walked to the driver's side, got in, and started the car. Monty sulked. But as the car pulled away, he realized the trip to the police station wasn't a total loss. He had learned about the cat burglar, and that could be just the break this case needed.

As for the rocks, he had a plan. He continued to pay close attention to the route.

Montgomery Schnauzer P.I. ────────────

Chapter Seven

Lost and Found

Monty was at the off-leash dog park again the next day. He was still in a funk after losing the only clue to his first case. But he had a plan to get those rocks back. He made a show of playing with the other dogs. When Sarah wasn't looking, Monty dashed away from the park.

Monty had always had a good sense of direction. His former master used to say that his initials, M.P.S., also stood for "Monty Positioning System". Monty paused, closed his eyes, and remembered the route from yesterday. It was as if he had a map in his mind. He knew exactly how to find the police station again. He set off at a trot.

Things were going great until Monty came to the first busy intersection. He needed to cross the street, but the constant stream of cars blocked his way. He waited for a break in the traffic, and waited, and waited, until he got dizzy from watching the whooshing cars.

A man arrived. He wore headphones over his ears and walked to the beat of music only he could hear. He didn't notice Monty. He half-walked, half-danced to the nearby pole, found a button there, and pressed it. The button beeped.

Monty looked at the button, then at the pole, then at the man. Was there a point to that? Monty wondered.

Lost and Found

Then something miraculous happened. The cars slowed to a stop in both directions. A path opened for Monty to cross. But he wasn't sure he should. Even stopped cars were dangerous. They could move at any time. Mr. Headphones Man strode across. He seemed confident, so Monty followed him.

They reached the other side safely. Monty jumped up on the sidewalk and resumed his run. He pulled away from the man in the headphones.

Monty came to another intersection. The sidewalk of the new street bustled with people. He closed his eyes to focus on the route. His memory told him to turn right. He opened his eyes and saw, with relief, that meant he did not have to cross another street. Monty turned right and joined the throng of people marching on the sidewalk.

"Oh dear! There's a lost little dog," Monty heard a woman's voice say. He looked around. He didn't see a lost dog.

"You need my help," the voice said.

Monty looked up. A portly woman with white hair stood over him. She clutched an enormous purse in one hand and reached for Monty with the other.

"Hey! I'm not lost," he barked. "I know exactly where I am."

"Come on, little fella," the woman said. "I need to get you to the animal shelter."

"Oh no!" Monty snarled at her. "No way! I'm not going back there!"

"Easy now; settle down," she cooed.

Monty growled and backed away. A few people stopped to watch. Monty could tell they wanted to help, but whose side were they on? Would they help him? Or would they help the old woman? Monty didn't have to wait long for an answer. The people formed a circle and trapped him inside.

Then Mr. Headphones Man came bopping around the corner.

The old woman called to him, "Is this your dog?"

Headphones Man ignored her.

Monty scurried to the man's side and said, "Yes, that's it. I'm his dog!"

Mr. Headphones paid no attention to him. Monty worried that no one would believe his little white lie. He stood on his hind legs and planted his front paws on the man.

"Hey, I'm talking to you," Monty said.

The man looked down and smiled. He took Monty's front paws in his hands, and gently swayed back and forth. Monty didn't expect to dance with him. He wanted to protest, but he saw the smile on the old woman's face. She believed.

"You really should keep your dog on a leash," she said to the man.

The woman waddled away. The not-so-helpful people also returned to whatever business brought them to this stretch of sidewalk.

Lost and Found

Monty followed Headphones Man as far as he could. Pretty soon though, the man's journey turned away from the police station. Monty had to risk traveling alone again. He had to get to that police station. His case depended on it.

He was almost there when the familiar big black vehicle showed up. It was the same car he had seen outside the coffee shop. It parked in front of Monty, right between him and the police station. The two police officers got out of the front. One of them reached for the back door. He was going to let the monster out!

The creature jumped out of the S.U.V. Monty saw that his detective instincts were right. This was no monster. In fact, it was a dog, a tall and stately dog with long coarse hair of black and brown. As the dog got close, Monty's nose told him much more. The dog was a girl, and she was in a very serious mood.

"Where is your person?" she asked. "Why are you wandering around alone?"

"I am looking for the police station," Monty said.

"Well, you found it. I am Constable Casey. You are in serious trouble, mister. Come with us at once!"

Monty assumed this had something to do with his case. Perhaps the cat burglar was on to him. Somehow the villain found out about Monty's investigation. He knew Monty would soon catch up to him and ruin his evil plan. That must mean Monty's life was in danger!

Lost and Found

One of the police officers clipped a leash on him.

Monty said, "I am Montgomery P. Schnauzer, private investigator. I appreciate your concern, but I can take care of myself."

"You're under arrest," said Casey.

"What?!" Monty could not believe what he just heard.

"I said, you're under arrest."

"On what charges?!"

"Vagrancy," she said. It seemed even police dogs liked big words.

Monty repeated it back to her, "*Vay gran see*... what does that mean?"

Lost and Found

"It means wandering around, off-leash, without your human. It's against the law."

"But I'm a detective! I'm on an important case. You must let me go." Monty was sure she would understand.

Instead, she read him his rights, "You have the right to remain silent. You have the right to have your human come collect you. If you don't have a human, one will be assigned to you from the animal shelter."

The police officers put him in the back of the vehicle. He barked in protest, but they ignored him. Casey jumped in the back, as well. The door closed. It was dark inside. Monty could not see out. He could not watch the route. Even if he got free, he would never be able to find his way back.

Montgomery Schnauzer P.I. ─────────────

He knew they would take him to jail, where they locked up all the bad guys. Monty felt a knot of fear in the pit of his stomach.

Chapter Eight

Hard Time

The place Monty ended up was worse than the animal shelter. They locked him in a bare cell with thick bars and no windows. The warden shut off the ugly ceiling lights after she locked him in here. The only light came through one grimy skylight in the ceiling. This place was a prison for dogs. They had treated him like a common criminal. On the ride over, he pleaded with Consta-*whatever* Casey. She proved to be most unreasonable. She didn't like freelance detectives, either. She made that point very clear. It was all so humiliating!

Fortunately, his cell mate was an agreeable fellow. He didn't look like much. He was a tiny dog, maybe all of five pounds if he were soaking wet. He had big ears, big eyes and a small nose. Yet he spoke well.

"What are you in for, amigo?" the little dog said.

Monty wanted to tell him, but he could not remember the fancy police word Casey used.

"Cat got your tongue, huh? That's OK. My name is Steve, but folks call me Little Houdini."

"Why do they call you that?" Monty asked.

"Because I have skills, special skills, skills that are useful in a place like this."

Monty stared, blinked twice, and stared some more. He didn't have the foggiest idea what the little dog was talking about.

"I'm an escape artist," Little Houdini explained.

"Really?" Monty asked, "Then how come you're stuck in here?"

"Well, the thing is..." the small dog stuttered; he seemed embarrassed. "I am big on talent, but short on... um... well, I'm short."

"I see," Monty said.

"But," Little Houdini continued, "if you give me a boost, I can get us both out of here."

Monty doubted his new friend had any talent at all, except maybe chasing dust bunnies under the couch. Still, he saw no harm in talking about escaping. They were stuck in here, after all. It wasn't like Monty had anything else to occupy his time.

"That only solves one of my problems," Monty said. "If I get out of here, I don't know where I am, or how to get from here to…" Monty couldn't finish that sentence. He'd almost revealed his plan. He wasn't sure he could trust Little Houdini. They had only met a few minutes ago — and in prison, of all places!

"To where, amigo? Where do you need to go?"

"Uh… home," Monty answered.

"Oh!" Houdini said, "That is easy, then. We must wait here. Your poppa will come, and he will take you home. That's how dog jail works. Did the police not read you your rights?"

Monty nodded, "Yes." He remembered Constable Casey going on and on about rights. The trouble was, Monty wasn't sure he had a human. Thinking of his master made him immediately sad. The last time Monty found himself in a predicament like this (at the animal shelter), his master had not come.

"Amigo?" Little Houdini said.

"No," Monty answered at last. "He is not coming."

"How about your momma, then?"

"I don't think I have a momma."

"Well then," Houdini said, "that settles it. We must get you out of here before someone comes to take you to the shelter. I will need that boost now."

"OK. Where do you want me?" Monty said.

"Over here, by the door."

Monty moved to the cage door. He bowed low to let Little Houdini climb on top of him. It felt really weird to have another dog standing on his back.

"Higher, amigo," Houdini said.

Monty stood up to his full height.

"That's it. Steady now."

Monty felt a shift in the weight on his back. Instead of four paws on his back, he felt only two. His new friend stretched up to put his front paws on the latch. He put one claw into it, fiddled around a bit, and then... CLICK! The door opened.

Hard Time

Very impressive, Monty thought.

Monty and his new friend sniffed their way around the prison block. They came to a big heavy door. Monty stood right in front of it. He expected Little Houdini to jump on his back again.

"Don't stand there, amigo," said the tiny dog. "When the door opens, it will break your nose."

Yikes, Monty thought, that sounds painful! He backed away.

Monty said, "I thought you would... you know..." He made a gesture with his paw, "Click?"

Houdini answered, "Not that door. It has a locking deadbolt. No dog can open that."

Monty didn't know what a locking deadbolt was, but it sounded like serious business. These special skills proved not so useful after all. They broke free of the cage only to remain trapped in the cell block.

"Well, how do we get through?" he asked.

"We wait for the humans to come. When they open the door, we scoot out."

Monty thought that was a crude plan for a so-called escape artist. He wondered if it would work. He went to the hinge-side of the door and hid against the wall, careful to keep his nose as far away from the door as he could.

"Not there either, " Houdini said. "You'll get trapped behind the door. Come over here with me."

Apparently, Monty had a lot to learn about escaping. He joined Little Houdini.

The small dog continued the lesson, "Stand still. Make no noises. Watch my tail, and wait for my signal. You must not go too early. The humans will see you. You must not go too late. The door will shut on you. Wait for my signal. When I go, you go."

Phew, Monty thought, this is tricky business! He followed Houdini's instructions. He stood still as a statue, staring at the other dog's tiny butt.

Moments passed like hours.

Finally, Monty heard footsteps in the room beyond the door. There were clomping footsteps, like someone in work boots, and clicking footsteps like someone in heels. The door swung open. The pair of work boots came through first, attached to a human in a khaki uniform. Monty watched Houdini for signs. The little dog stood rigid. Then the high heels came through, attached to a woman's legs under a pretty dress.

"Now!" said Houdini's tail. The little dog dashed through the door.

Monty followed. His whiskers brushed the hem of the woman's skirt. His nose caught a whiff of something pleasant. He didn't place it until after the door closed behind him with a clang. The scent was strawberry perfume.

Little Houdini and Monty were in a brightly lit room with a high counter and a few uncomfortable looking chairs. To Monty this looked like another one of the rooms that humans called a lobby. Houdini ran toward a pair of glass doors. Outside was the street, and trees, and clear blue sky.

"Hurry," the small dog urged. "Help me open this last door."

Monty stood frozen. He knew that smell. That was Sarah.

"Amigo, now! The door!"

Monty mumbled, "She came..."

"By now the warden has seen our empty cage! She will come back any second!"

The cell block door opened.

"Hide!" Little Houdini said, and pushed Monty toward the chairs.

Monty had to crouch to squeeze under the nearest chair. Houdini simply walked under. They managed to hide in the nick of time. Sarah came through the door, followed by the warden.

"I'm sure I latched that cage," the warden said.

"You're sure he was here? A little gray Schnauzer?" Sarah asked.

Monty could tell Sarah was annoyed. He heard that tone in her voice a lot.

"I keep telling you: yes," the warden said, "and a Chihuahua, and they're both gone."

Sarah shrugged and said, "You're the animal control expert."

Monty whispered to Little Houdini, "What if she is my momma? I have to go to her."

"Are you sure?" Houdini asked. "How do you know she is not here to take you to the animal shelter?"

"I don't," Monty replied.

Houdini raised his little eyebrows.

Monty continued, "This is the only way to find out. You should stay here. Wherever she takes me, we need to go out that door. When it opens, you can scoot free."

Monty wiggled forward. He felt a tiny paw come to rest on his flank. He stopped.

"Amigo," Houdini spoke, "let me go first. Let me take the blame for our breakout."

"What? No. I can't ruin your chance to get free."

"I can get free again. Besides, my poppa will come for me. He always does. He loves me. He will forgive me for yet another escape. You don't know where you stand with your human. You don't need to add 'prison break' to your rap sheet!"

"Are you sure?" Monty asked.

Houdini nodded, "Yes. If we are to keep you out of the animal shelter, we must make you seem, as much as possible, as though you are still a good dog."

With that last statement, the tiny dog marched bravely out from under the chair. The warden noticed him immediately. Houdini ran from her. He capered around the room, barking madly.

"Ha ha, copper!" he barked, "Your cages will never hold Little Houdini! Never! Bah ha ha ha ha!"

A lump formed in Monty's throat as he considered what Houdini said. In truth, Monty did not know where he stood with Sarah. Maybe he already had too many strikes against him. Maybe Sarah didn't want to take him home again. Oh well, it was too late to change his mind now. Houdini had revealed their position – in his overly dramatic style.

Monty gulped. He wiggled out from under the chair.

Houdini saw him. The little Chihuahua gave Monty a wink, then stopped running. He let the warden grab him. As he lay in the woman's arms, he pantomimed a fake death scene.

"Ohhhh! She got me," Houdini howled. "It's all over! I'm done for! Gah!" And he collapsed, his head hanging from the warden's arm like a rag doll.

Monty approached Sarah, her attention on the conclusion of the absurd cop-and-robber chase scene. He nuzzled the back of her leg with his nose. She spun around, startled.

He asked, "You're not going to take me back to the shelter, are you?"

Sarah didn't answer. She clipped the leash on him.

Little Houdini lifted his head and whispered, "Stay free, my friend!"

Monty rode in silence in the passenger seat of Sarah's car. He hoped they were headed home to Sarah's house. Monty did not know where he belonged in the new scheme of things, but he knew for sure he did not want to go back to that shelter.

Sarah said, "I'm taking you to visit my friend Wendy. She is a dog whisperer. Maybe she can help me with you."

A dog whisperer! Monty thought that was terrific. Certainly, she would understand him.

Chapter Nine
A Little Tied Up

"Rise and shine, sleepy-head," Sarah said, as she pulled the blinds open to let the sunlight in.

Monty squinted. It was too early to get up for a normal day. And this was not a normal day. Yesterday's adventure really wore him out. He felt like a living example of the expression "dog tired." If this arrangement was going to work at all, she would have to understand he was not a morning person.

"If this arrangement is going to work at all," she said, "we need help."

No, he thought, what we need is more sleep.

Sarah continued, "I don't have Wendy's phone number. We'll have to go to the park early to make sure we don't miss her."

A half hour later, they were dressed, leashed and walking to the dog park. They arrived to find the park empty. They were the first ones there. Monty was not impressed. He could have slept more. He decided he should use this opportunity to sniff around for more clues. He looked up at Sarah, expecting her to disconnect the leash. She didn't.

"You're staying on-leash, mister," she said. "I can't trust you."

Now that's a laugh, he thought. She's the untrustworthy one. She's the one who lost his only clue at the police station. He was too tired to argue. He plunked himself down on the grass and let out a yawn.

Monty watched the park. It wasn't as empty as it seemed. Crows hopped and flitted around the edges, looking for food scraps dropped the day before. Squirrels crisscrossed the grass, going about their mysterious squirrel business. As interesting as all this was, he was still sleepy. He had to fight the urge to doze off.

Licky and Sticky arrived on the scene, barking. The squirrels and crows scattered into the trees. The Pug twins raced over to Monty.

"Hey, Mr. Detective!" said one.

"How goes the investigation?" said the other.

Monty had not forgotten which dog was which, but he needed to get a good smell to tell them apart. He got up and walked to the back-end of the nearest Pug.

"Oh..." he said between sniffs, "Hi... Sticky. Hi Licky. Not good, I'm afraid. I'm stuck on-leash."

"That sucks, dog," Licky said.

"Can we help somehow?" Sticky asked.

Monty thought for a bit. He didn't know how long this new on-leash policy would last. It would make it difficult to get any investigating done. The detectives in books often used informants to find out what went on in secret places. That's what I need, he thought. The Pug twins weren't exactly *Baker Street Irregulars*, but they did have a knack for sticking their flat, little noses in everyone's

A Little Tied Up

business. They probably knew a lot about what went on in this neighborhood.

Monty asked, "How would you like to be informants?"

"Oh wow!"

"That would be awesome!"

The twins' excitement faded fast. The same puzzled look crept over each dog's face.

"Um... what does that mean?" Sticky asked.

"It means that you tell me what's going on in places I can't get to," Monty explained. "Can you be my eyes and ears for a while?"

"Shouldn't we use our noses?" Licky asked.

"Well... uh," Monty said. "Yes. Of course." The question threw him off. He had to think about it for a bit. Then he said, "Eyes and ears is just an expression we detectives use. It reminds us to use all our senses. Not just our noses."

"Oh," the Pugs nodded in unison, "that makes sense."

Sarah waited on a park bench with her legs crossed. She yawned and wished she'd stopped to get a coffee beforehand. Monty mingled around those two weird Pugs she'd seen many times since she started going out with her new dog. Their owner stood on the far side of the park, focused on his phone and not paying any attention to his dogs. Finally, Wendy showed up with her dog, Jiff.

"Hi Wendy! I need to talk to you." Sarah said. She tried not to sound desperate.

"Sure, Sarah. What's up?"

"It's Monty. He's out of control! I don't know what to do. I think I am going to have to take him back to the shelter."

Monty hadn't paid any attention to the humans. But as he exchanged pleasantries with Jiff, the last bit Sarah said caught his ear. Little Houdini was right. She really did want to take him back to the shelter. He could not let that happen. But what could he do?

The women traded leashes. Sarah took Jiff's lead, and Wendy took Monty's. She gave it a tug.

"Come, Monty," Wendy said.

Monty resisted. This woman was definitely not his momma. He felt certain she would to take him back to the shelter.

"Monty, come." the woman said firmly.

No way. Unh-uh. Not going to happen. Monty did not move. Wendy pulled on the leash. He dug his paws into the sod. Sarah stood still, watching. Wendy waved her away.

"Go ahead," Wendy said to Sarah.

Sarah walked away with Jiff following obediently.

Monty howled, "Noooooooo!"

"Come!" Wendy ordered and yanked the leash.

A Little Tied Up

Monty didn't have any choice. He plodded after her.

Chapter Ten

Miss Communication

To Monty's relief, they did not go to the animal shelter. Instead, they walked all over the neighborhood. They were "practicing". That's what Wendy said. Monty could not imagine what they were practicing for. He had to come, sit, stay, even lift a paw so Wendy could shake it. None of it seemed to have any purpose. The worst one was a game called "heel". It involved following very close to the human holding the leash. Monty had no room to roam. He couldn't investigate any of the tempting smells as they passed by.

His detective reasoning told him that all this practicing was keeping him out of the animal shelter. So he played along.

Wendy passed the leash back to Sarah. Finally, all this nonsense was over!

"Now you try," said Wendy.

Monty rolled his eyes. The practicing started all over again. This time, Sarah had the leash and gave the commands. Monty acted quickly each time. He wanted to get these stupid games over with.

At long last, they arrived at Jiff's home. Monty wondered if this was the end of the meeting. He never got a chance to talk to

Miss Communication

this human who was supposed to be able to understand dog language!

Wendy invited them upstairs. They went into the building. It was so much like the building where Sarah lived. It even had a magic room. What were the odds of that? Monty wondered. And like Sarah's building, this magic room took them to a hallway with lots of doors. Wendy and Jiff found the one that belonged to them. They all went inside.

"Be careful of Fritz," Jiff warned with fear in his voice.

"What's a Fritz?" Monty asked.

"He is a ninja cat."

This caught Monty's attention. A cat! Not just any cat, either. This one had expert martial arts training.

Wendy grabbed a towel hanging inside the door and used it to wipe Jiff's paws. Without even asking, she also wiped Monty's paws. He wanted to protest, but thought the better of it. This might be his only chance to convey a message to the humans. He waited until her eyes met his, then he used his most expressive stare.

"Wendy the Whisper Woman," Monty said, "listen to me. I am a detective. You have to explain this to Sarah. She does not understand."

"He likes to look you right in the eyes," Wendy said to Sarah.

Miss Communication

Monty tried again, "No, Wendy, listen. Explain to Sarah that I am a detective."

"That's unusual for a dog," Wendy continued.

"You don't really speak dog, do you?" Monty said.

"Oh, you're so cute!" Wendy said to him, and she patted him on the head.

Monty was flabbergasted. This was an obvious waste of time. He decided to get back to his investigation, and that meant talking to this ninja cat, Fritz. Monty knew the burglar was a cat. And here was a cat with all the skills needed to pull off a daring heist. Monty had identified his first suspect. He followed Jiff into the living room.

"Where would I find this cat?" Monty asked.

Jiff pointed with his nose toward the couch. On the back of the couch lay a long-haired black cat. It eyed the dogs with malice. Monty strode confidently toward the cat.

"Monty, no!" Jiff said.

"Hey cat," Monty said, "I want to talk to you."

The cat said nothing. Its eyes narrowed. Its tail twitched.

Jiff pleaded, "Monty, leave him alone! He's a bad kitty!"

"Is that so?" Monty said. "All the more reason to question him."

Monty stood on his back legs and put his front paws as high up the couch as he could reach. The cat turned away and twitched its

Miss Communication

tail even more. Monty got the impression Fritz was trying to ignore him.

"You are rude, mister cat," Monty said.

At last, Fritz spoke, "You should have listened to your friend."

The cat moved so fast Monty's eyes couldn't follow it.

Whap! Whap! Whap! A flurry of black paws struck Monty's face. Then the cat bounded down Monty's back. At the bottom, it gave a kick. Monty smacked into the couch. He scrambled to his feet and spun around.

"You dirty cat!" barked Monty.

Fritz had vanished. Monty looked left and then right. He saw Jiff trying to hide

Miss Communication

under an end table, but no cat. He heard a scream above him.

"Hi-yeow!"

A black streak leapt from a shelf and landed on the end table. The cat leapt again. Jiff scampered out from under the table, knocking a lamp flying. The cat landed on Monty.

"Yipe!" he squealed in pain.

The lamp crashed to the floor. Monty whipped around and snapped his jaws. The cat kicked away, safely avoiding Monty's bite.

"Too slow!" Fritz taunted.

Sarah and Wendy ran into the living room just as Jiff ran out. He ran past Sarah and headlong into Wendy, knocking her off her feet. Sarah stepped into the room. She saw

Monty round the couch, barking, as the cat ran up and over it.

"Mrraaow!" screeched the cat.

It pounced on Monty as he ran by, and bowled him over. The cat grabbed hold and tumbled with him, biting and scratching.

"Stop it! Stop!" shouted Sarah. She reached for the cat.

"Don't!" Wendy said. "He'll cut you to shreds."

Sarah pulled back. Wendy arrived with a water bottle. She squirted cold water on both Fritz and Monty.

"Hisssss!" said Fritz. He shot Wendy a death-stare and darted under the couch.

Miss Communication

Sarah went to Monty. He lay on his side, panting. He was covered with scratches and cuts.

"Oh you poor thing," Sarah said.

Wendy put her hand on Sarah's shoulder and said, "We should take him to the pet hospital."

Chapter Eleven

Exaggerated Reports

Monty and Sarah arrived late at the dog park the next day. Monty had stitches and bandages and a funny taste in his mouth from the medicine she had put in his food. Sarah kept him on-leash the whole time. He didn't mind so much. His body ached all over. He didn't feel up to running around.

He caused quite a stir when he showed up. All the dogs came running over to see him. Licky and Sticky led the pack.

"Dude!" Licky said, "We heard what happened."

"Did you really take on Fritz the Ninja Cat?" Sticky asked.

Another dog said, "Of course! Look at the bandages."

"Well, I heard he was dead!" came a familiar female voice. "Let me through. I want to talk to him."

Monty recognized the caramel colors of Duchess as she pushed her way through the crowd.

"Where the bark have you been?!" she demanded. "I thought we were going to track the scent of the bone thief."

"Well," Monty said, "There have been... um... other developments."

"I can see that. You're no longer allowed off-leash. Fine detective you turned out to be!" Duchess said.

"That won't be a problem. I've got help." Monty said, and he nodded to the Pug twins.

"Oh please! Those two clowns couldn't find their own tails if they had a map."

"Hey!" said Licky and Sticky together.

Monty was anxious to change the track this conversation was on. He said, "Actually, the development is: I have a lead on a suspect. The thief," he paused for effect, "is a cat."

Gasps of shock went through the crowd. Even Duchess was left speechless. When the other dogs spoke again, it was in hushed tones.

Duchess collected her thoughts and said, "It was Fritz, wasn't it? He stole my bone, that demon cat."

"Well, he's a suspect. Maybe he had something to do with it, and maybe he didn't."

"Sounds like you don't know a lot."

"I'm working on it," he said through clenched teeth. She had some attitude! Monty spent a night in jail and fought for his life against a vicious cat. She could show a little appreciation.

"Humph!" she said in disgust and strode off.

She paused, turned her head back and added, "I'm glad you're not dead."

Then she was gone.

Sarah regretted bringing Monty to the dog park. If she'd known the other dogs would mob him, she never would have brought him here. The veterinarian had told her to keep Monty rested.

"A little help, please," she called to the other dog owners. "He's got stitches. I need to get him out of here."

"Lady, you shouldn't have brought him here," someone said.

"Yes, I see that now." Sarah was annoyed, but she tried not to show it.

The other humans pulled their dogs away. Sarah reached in and lifted Monty up into her arms. Some of the dogs barked and lunged at Monty. She turned her back to them. Out of the corner of her eye, she could have sworn one of the Pug twins winked. She looked over her shoulder. Both Pugs sat, looking up at her. They seemed to be smiling, although she doubted such a thing was possible for a dog.

Aside from the trip to the park, the day was uneventful. Sarah did not let Monty do much, and that suited him just fine. Later that evening, he settled down to sleep on the comfy human bed. Heaven help him, he did love that bed!

In the middle of the night, Monty awoke with a start. It must have been a noise, he thought. But what was it? Where had it come from? He looked around. Sarah was sound asleep under the covers. He was about to put his head back down when he heard it again.

"Mrraaow!"

It was a screech, definitely from a cat, probably in a fight. Monty shuddered, recalling the beating he had suffered at the claws of Fritz the Ninja Cat.

"Meeeerrraow!"

The sound was not close, and it was definitely outside somewhere. He got up and walked over

Sarah to get to the edge of the bed. He jumped down and went to the window. He pushed the blinds aside with his head so he could see outside. In the pale glow of the streetlights, the neighboring buildings looked like standing giants. But he could not see the cat fight.

Sarah stirred.

"Huh? What's the matter?" she said; her voice sounded croaky.

Monty said, "I heard something outside. Did you hear it too?"

He moved to a different spot, sending the blinds swaying. The new spot wasn't any better than the last one. He figured the fighting cat was somewhere behind, or maybe in, one of the buildings.

"Good grief," she said. "Don't tell me you need a bathroom break at this hour?"

Monty shot her a look that said, "Shush! I'm trying to listen."

He pricked up his ears and pressed closer to the window. She sat up and turned on the bedside lamp. Now it was brighter inside than out. He couldn't see anything at all.

Sarah left the room. She made a lot of noise, rummaging in the hall closet. For someone who told him to shush a lot, Sarah didn't seem to understand the concept herself. She returned a moment later wearing a coat over her pajamas and a pair of untied running shoes on her feet.

"Come on," she said. She let out a big yawn and then added, "Let's go."

He followed her out of the bedroom, through the living room, and out the apartment door. They stood in the hall and waited for the sliding door to open to the magic room.

She said, " We're not making a habit of this, you know."

"I should hope not," he replied. "I don't want to go chasing dangerous criminals in the middle of the night any more than you do."

The door slid open. The bright lights in the elevator hurt his sleepy eyes. He had to squint to look up at Sarah. He noticed her squinting also. The door closed, and the elevator did its magic trick. It opened again at the building lobby. They walked across the smooth tiled floor to the glass doors that led outside. Sarah held one of the doors open.

ExaggeratedReports

Monty took a few nervous steps. His eyes had finally adjusted to the indoor light. Now the outdoors looked especially dark and scary.

"Go on," Sarah said. "Do your business."

Right, Monty thought. He listened intently for any signs of that cat. He moved cautiously, afraid that any moment Fritz would leap out of the bushes. He followed the cobblestone path around the building, pausing often to sniff and listen.

"Will you hurry up? I want to go back to bed." She sounded annoyed.

"Shush!" he glared back, annoyed.

Their little walk brought them back to the main doors of the building. Monty had not heard the cat screech again. Nor had he

Montgomery Schnauzer P.I.

ExaggeratedReports

smelled any fresh cat odors. He strode away from the doors, intending to search the next building over. Sarah grabbed him by the back of his collar.

"Oh no you don't," she said. "We're going back to bed."

And that's what they did. Moments later, Monty was on top of the comfy human bed, and Sarah was tucked under the sheets.

"I don't know what I'm going to do with you, dog," she said.

Monty stared at the window and listened. He heard Sarah's breathing change to a slow, deep rhythm. He knew she was asleep. Still he listened.

Eventually, and in spite of himself, he fell asleep.

Monty had a strange dream. In it, Fritz the Ninja Cat climbed up the building and broke in through the patio door. Monty found the cat in the kitchen, eating all the food. Monty barked and the cat turned. It suddenly grew to be six feet tall – and pounced!

Montgomery Schnauzer P.I. ─────────────

Chapter Twelve
Word on the Street

Monty awoke stiff and sore.

Sarah noticed him stirring. "You must have had quite the dream."

"It was a nightmare," Monty said. "I need to talk to my informants. I have a feeling the cat burglar was on the prowl last night."

Monty didn't expect a response. He was used to the fact that she didn't understand him. She lifted him down from the bed.

"Come on," she said. "Let's go make breakfast."

That seemed like a fine plan to him. He worked better on a full stomach.

After breakfast, Sarah took Monty for their morning walk. But she didn't take him to the dog park. This upset him. How was he supposed to find Licky and Sticky? Instead, they went around the block and ended up at the coffee shop. Sarah made Monty wait outside (again), and she went in to get her drink. While she was gone, Jiff and Wendy showed up.

"Oh look, Jiff. It's Monty," Wendy said.

"Hi Monty!" Jiff said, wagging his tail. "My name is Jiff."

"Hi Jiff," Monty said.

Word on the Street

"How are you feeling little buddy?" Wendy said as she bent down to pet him.

"Sore," Monty said.

"You must be sore, poor thing."

Yup, Monty thought, that's what I said. He turned to Jiff and asked, "Tell me. Was Fritz at home last night?"

"I don't know," Jiff said. "I was at Grandma's all night. Have you ever been to Grandma's? It is just the best!"

Inside the coffee shop, Sarah waited for her sugar-free vanilla soy latte. Wendy came in, ordered a coffee, and then came over to talk to her.

"I'm sorry my cat was such a jerk," Wendy said. "Is Monty OK?"

Sarah said, "The vet said he will be fine; just to take it easy with him. I'm not sure it was all Fritz's fault. We were there for dog training lessons, after all."

Sarah noticed her friend did not seem to be her usual happy self.

"Are you OK, Wendy? You look stressed."

"Oh, I'm fine," Wendy said. "It's just, well, I spent the night at my mom's. When I got home this morning, I found my apartment ransacked."

"What?! Was anything taken?"

"Not a thing. Isn't that weird? I think maybe someone came in through the patio door, and Fritz did to him what he did to Monty."

Sarah laughed and said, "Are you suggesting some hardened criminal climbed up the side of your building, but couldn't get past your attack cat?"

Wendy looked hurt for a second, then her expression softened and she laughed as well.

"I know it sounds crazy," Wendy said, "but I came home to the aftermath of a war zone, nothing missing, and Mr. Fritz sitting pretty-as-you-please on the back of the couch. If you have another explanation, I'm all ears."

Sarah said, "I guess only your cat knows for sure. It's too bad animals can't talk."

Montgomery Schnauzer P.I.

Word on the Street

Back outside, Monty said to Jiff, "Yes, yes, Grandma's house sounds fantastic. But what about Fritz? Was he locked in the apartment? Could he have gotten out somehow?"

Jiff thought about that question for a long while before he replied, "Well, Momma left the back door open so he could go out on the patio if he wanted."

"Ah-ha!" Monty said. "I bet Fritz climbed down from that patio."

The evidence was building against Fritz the Ninja Cat. He could have been out last night. The next step would be to figure out who the other fighter was. Somewhere out there was the victim, the poor creature that Fritz attacked. But this was a big city. Finding that creature could be tough. Monty now

Word on the Street

understood why story detectives tried to get what they called "the word on the street." Again, Monty was reminded that he needed to talk to his informants.

Monty asked, "Have you seen Licky and Sticky?"

"Yes," Jiff said, "I see them right now."

The Pug twins came around the corner, pulling on their leashes. They seemed to be dragging their man behind them. He hung on to the leashes with one hand and a cell phone with the other.

"There's that dog!" said Licky, "Hey Mister Detective, we've been looking for you!"

"Oh good, Jiff is here too," Sticky said. "Now we'll get the whole story."

The two Pugs beamed with excitement. Their curly tails wagged in anticipation. They waited for Monty to speak. When he didn't, they turned to Jiff. They looked him over as if they had just noticed something out-of-place in his appearance.

"Hey," Licky said. "He's in one piece."

"How come you're not all beaten up?" Sticky asked of Jiff.

Jiff blinked.

Monty asked, "Why would he be beaten up?"

Licky responded, "Because of the big fight."

"Oh good," Monty said. "You know something about the fight."

Word on the Street

"Well, yeah." Sticky said. "We live in the apartment next door to Jiff and Fritz. We heard the whole thing. Fritz went all ninja-kitty on... uh..."

"Someone," Licky said, finishing his brother's thought. "But, if it wasn't Jiff, then whom?"

"Indeed," Monty said, "our friend Jiff has an alibi."

"What's an al-uh-bye?" Sticky asked.

"Alibi is a detective's word. It means that Jiff has proof he was not present during the big cat fight. He was elsewhere when it happened."

Jiff felt he finally had something to add to the conversation. "Oh, yes! I was at Grandma's house. Have you been to Grandma's house? It is awesome!"

"Oh no," Monty groaned, "here he goes again."

Before Jiff could launch into another rousing description of all that was great about Grandma's house, Wendy and Sarah came out of the shop.

Sarah said to Wendy, "You will report your burglary to the police, right?"

"But nothing was taken, so it wasn't really a burglary."

"Someone was in your house, Wendy. That's still a crime. It was probably that cat burglar. It might seem like nothing to you, but you might have clues the police need to catch him."

Word on the Street

Monty perked up. "Guys," he addressed the other dogs, "do you realize what this means? Fritz is not the cat burglar!"

"He has an al-uh-bye, too?" Licky asked.

"Not exactly. An alibi would be if Fritz were not there. But he was there, in his own home, when the real thief tried to rob it."

In an odd turn of events, Jiff caught on before the Pug twins. This was not like him at all.

Jiff said, "So, it was the cat burglar that Fritz beat up?"

Monty nodded, "Yes."

Licky laughed, which through his pushed-in nose came out as a snort. "Oh," he said, "the stupid cat burglar chose the wrong house to mess with!"

Monty nodded.

Sticky said, "And Fritz beat him up and sent him running away."

Monty nodded.

Chapter Thirteen
Therapy Dog

Monty wondered what this new information meant to his case. The ninja cat had been his best suspect! Actually, the cat was his only suspect. Now he had proof that Fritz was not the thief. The trail had gone cold. And without that all-important bag of rocks, he didn't know how to pick it up again.

Licky asked, "Are you coming to the dog park, Monty?"

"I don't think so. Sarah wants me to go to something called a therapy dog tryout."

"What's that? You're going to try to get therapy?"

"No, no. The humans go to the hospital to get therapy. Special dogs go to cheer up the humans. It helps them get better faster."

"Do you get treats for that?" Licky asked.

"I'm sure you'd get treats for that, Licky!" Sticky said.

Jiff said, "I like treats."

Sticky said, "I want to be a therapy dog!"

Licky said, "Me too!"

Monty rolled his eyes and said, "Well, it's the last thing I want to do. I'm on an important case, remember? I'm not going to find any clues at the human hospital. This will be a big waste of time."

By now, Wendy and Sarah had finished their conversation. They said goodbye. Sarah tugged on Monty's leash.

"Come, Monty," she said.

He cast his friends a reluctant see-you-later look. Then he trotted after her. She led him back to their building and into the magic room. When the sliding door opened again, they were in the park-in-garage.

Sarah set off across the unpleasant concrete floor with Monty in tow. Soon they arrived at her car. She loaded Monty into the passenger seat and plopped herself in the driver's seat. When she turned the key, the car did not start. Instead it complained.

"Rurrrr, rurrrr, rurrrr," said the car.

"Stupid car," Sarah said. She tried the key again.

"Rurrrr, rurrrr, rurrrr, rurrrr, vrurp!"

Monty could understand many animals, but the language of cars baffled him. He guessed the car was saying, "I don't want to." Mostly, that guess was based on the fact the car did not move.

"Rur-rurrrr vrurp, rur-rurrrr vrurp, rur-rurrrr vrurp."

"Not now," Sarah said. "We're going to be late."

The car must have understood that, because it started at last.

"Vroom!"

Then they were off. Sarah drove the car through the city streets. Before long they were out of the neighborhood and in unfamiliar territory.

They arrived at an outdoor park for cars. Sarah took Monty out of the car. They walked for a while and came to a big, white building. When they got close, the front doors opened automatically. Monty thought that was a neat trick.

Even though he knew he would find nothing at the human hospital to help his case, he felt he ought to investigate anyway. His nose picked up a lot of medicine scents. It smelled like a veterinary clinic, which put him on edge. He liked his old vet. She always had cookies in her pocket. But his new vet poked him with needles and gave him stitches. Monty would never forget that.

Of course, this place was not a veterinary clinic. For a start, it was much larger. The huge lobby stretched out before him like some stainless, white cavern. Several hallways branched off, leading to the deeper reaches of the building. And there were no animals here; only humans, an awful lot of humans. A few of them knew Sarah. They waved to her, and greeted her by name.

"Now Monty," Sarah said to get his attention, "I work here, alright. Don't do anything to embarrass me."

Monty missed her meaning entirely. As far as he was concerned, he'd never done anything embarrassing. The times she got upset with him in the past seemed to be over nothing. He followed Sarah to a big counter, where she stopped to talk to a woman with puffy red hair and wing-tipped glasses.

"Hi, Roxanne," she said.

"Oh hi, Sarah! Are you coming back to work?"

"Um... no, not yet. I am here for the therapy dog tryout." Sarah held up the end of the leash.

"They're meeting in the visitor lounge; down the hall and to the right," Roxanne said, and she leaned over the counter to look at Monty. "Oh what a cute little Schnauzer! He'll do fine. The patients are going to love him."

"Thank you," Sarah said to the woman, and then to Monty, "Come on, boy."

Monty followed a short way until something else caught his attention. This something made his tummy sink and his hair stand up. It was a scent that smelled exactly like Fritz the Ninja Cat. Monty cast a fearful look over his shoulder, expecting to see Fritz coming after him. Instead he saw a man walk up to the counter. This man was dressed all in black. His clothes had cat hair on them, and that cat hair smelled like Fritz. He also had deep scratches, bad enough to bleed. This man must be the burglar that Fritz beat up!

Wait, what? Monty thought. A man?!

That didn't make sense. Monty had been certain the cat burglar was, well, a cat. Yet here before him was a man, who had, without a doubt, Fritz-induced injuries. Monty recalled the teachings of Sherlock Holmes: "Eliminate all which is impossible, then whatever remains, however improbable, must be the truth." As weird as it seemed, there was only one explanation. The thief was not a cat, but rather a man pretending to be a cat.

Monty's anger flared, overcoming his initial fear. If he'd been able to keep those rocks, he would have tracked this man and caught him already. Monty resolved not to let the villain slip away this time. He charged at him.

"Stop! Thief!" he barked. "Hold it right th—"

A sudden jerk caught Monty's throat. He'd reached the end of his leash. Stupid leash, he thought. It ruined a perfectly good sneak attack. The man slunk away into the crowd. Monty could no longer see him. But he was sure he could find him, if he could just get over there.

Monty barked to Sarah, "Let me go! That's the bad guy! I have to get him!"

"Monty, shush!" Sarah said.

"No! You don't understand! He's getting away!"

Therapy Dog

Sarah was at her wits' end. Monty picked the worst time and place to pitch a barking fit, here at the hospital where she used to work and hoped to return. He caused a huge scene. Everyone stared. Surely they all wondered, can't that woman control her dog? Sarah dragged Monty out of there, while he barked frantically.

"Bark! Bark-bark-bark! Bark! Bark! Bark-bark!"

"Monty, quiet!" she yelled.

Once she got him back through the front doors and outside, he calmed down. He stopped barking. Instead, he looked from side to side and growled.

"What did I tell you?!" Sarah scolded. "Why can't you be a good dog?!"

She managed to get him into the car without further incident. She drove in silence while Monty sulked in the passenger seat. After she had calmed down, she let out a big sigh.

She said, "This is clearly not working out. I will keep you until your wounds heal, and then you're going back to the shelter."

Sarah was certain he could not understand her. So why did his little face suddenly look sad?

Montgomery Schnauzer P.I. ───────────

Chapter Fourteen
Hatching A Plan

By the next day, Monty slid into a depression. He had been so close to catching the thief and solving the case. But the man/cat burglar had slipped away. Monty had also lost his off-leash privileges, probably forever, and that made it really difficult to go sniffing around for clues. He didn't know what to do. He thought that maybe he was not a great detective after all.

The worst part was that Sarah did not want him any more.

He liked his new place in Sarah's house. True, it was not the home he'd grown up in. He missed his beloved master terribly. But Monty realized now that his man was truly gone. He wanted to believe the man would come back. However, Monty's detective side knew otherwise. He had processed the evidence. His master loved him. Monty knew that, as any dog who has been loved knows. His man would never have left Monty in the shelter all that time. If it were possible for him to come back, he would have.

Instead, it was Sarah who came to rescue him. She took him in, fed him, and cared for him. She even let him sleep on her bed. This could have been his new home. But Monty ruined it. If only he had caught that burglar!

Hatching A Plan

Sarah would have been proud of him. She would want to be his momma.

Sarah took him out, as she always did, but it wasn't their typical fun and social affair. She led him to the street-side of the building, so he could do his business on the strip of grass beside the road. The whooshing cars made him uncomfortable, but the need to pee was more uncomfortable. He didn't complain. He just did his business. He was trying his best to be a good dog for Sarah.

Back at the apartment, Sarah cleaned up the breakfast dishes while Monty wandered into the living room. He lay down in a warm patch of sun to think for a bit. How could he turn this situation around? Before long, the warmth made him sleepy. As he lay there fighting the desire to close his eyes, he overheard Sarah talking on the phone.

"Yes, well, I adopted a dog, but it's not working out," she said.

Monty jerked awake. He did not like the sound of that.

"How do I return him to the shelter?"

Monty's heart raced. This was it! Any minute now, she would collect him and take him back to the shelter. He ran for it. He tried to get as far from Sarah as he could. That put him in the bedroom. He hid in the closet.

If she can't find me, he thought, she can't take me back.

The bottom of the closet was crowded with shoes and boxes. He couldn't get in very far.

Hatching A Plan

When she came into the bedroom, she found him immediately.

"There you are," she said.

Monty squirmed away from her. He tried to wedge himself behind the stack of boxes. He couldn't fit. One of the boxes tumbled over, dumping its contents on the floor. Sarah gasped in shock. He leapt over the spilled box and sprinted out of the bedroom.

He ran back to the living room. He scanned around for a another hiding spot. He crawled under an end table and sat down. He waited with his ears pricked, listening for any sounds of activity from Sarah.

For the longest time, he heard nothing. Then he heard soft sobbing coming from the bedroom. He left his hiding place, stopped,

Montgomery Schnauzer P.I.

Hatching A Plan

and listened some more. Then he crept ever so slowly back to the bedroom.

He found Sarah sitting on the floor by the spilled box. She had photographs spread all around her. She also held one in her hand. She was crying. Monty didn't understand her change in mood. She had seemed so stern earlier. Monty knew one thing, though. Sarah needed him. It took him a moment to suppress his fear that she would take him to the shelter. He then walked slowly forward and sat beside her, as close as he could get without touching.

He stared at her with his soft brown eyes. Sarah reached out her hand and stroked his head.

She said, "You and I have something in common, I guess. We've both been abandoned."

Hatching A Plan

In that moment, Monty realized that she had, in a way, understood him. Not so much by the things he had said over the past several days. She understood his emotion. To a dog that was the important part anyway. They had come to a place where both of them experienced the same feeling at the same time. Monty rested his head on her leg.

He could not say how long they stayed there. Sarah continued to pet him, running her hand over his head and down his back in long strokes. He felt content, and she stopped crying. Eventually, she spoke.

"You know," Sarah said, "Duchess is having a birthday party,"

What's a birthday party? Monty wondered.

Montgomery Schnauzer P.I.

Hatching A Plan

"Isn't that the dumbest thing? A birthday party for a dog!"

So it's a dumb thing, he thought. He would ignore it then.

"Her... uh... parents, I guess... invited us. Maybe we should go. I could use some social time."

Oh no! Monty thought. He put together enough from what she said. They were expected to visit Duchess. Monty definitely did not want that. Duchess was his client, and he'd failed her. How could he face her now?

Sarah said, "Come on. We can't stay in this closet forever. It's time to take you for a walk."

Monty dragged his feet on the walk. His heart wasn't into it. He didn't even get excited when Sarah took him to the dog park. He hadn't been there since the morning after his battle with Fritz the Ninja Cat. He should have been thrilled. They went to Sarah's favorite bench. Monty took his place at her feet. He watched the other dogs running around, enjoying themselves.

"Oh, all right," Sarah said. "I feel bad for you."

She reached down and removed his leash.

"Thank you," Monty said with a look. Yet he stayed put.

Licky and Sticky arrived, all excited. They came up to Monty.

"What's wrong?" Sticky asked.

Hatching A Plan

"Yeah," Licky said, "aren't you excited about the party?"

"I heard a dog party is the dumbest thing," Monty said.

"What?!" the twins said at the same time.

"I think Mr. Detective here needs a lesson in partying!" Licky said to his brother. They both looked like they were going to burst out laughing.

"Here's what goes down at a birthday party," Sticky explained. "All the dogs and the humans get together and eat cake."

"Cake!" Licky said. "Does that sound dumb to you?"

Monty had to agree. That didn't sound dumb at all. In fact, it improved his mood greatly. It wasn't the thought of eating cake that made him happier. Though he had to admit that would be a nice bonus. What got his spirits up was an idea, a most fabulous idea.

"Come on, you guys," Monty said. "I need your help. We need to deliver a message to every dog who's going to be at that party."

Sarah watched Monty interacting with the two Pugs. To her surprise, he left his spot at her feet. Monty ran from dog to dog, with the Pug twins at his heels. He seemed happier. Sarah let out a sigh of relief.

Chapter Fifteen
The Party

Later that evening, Monty and Sarah walked to the party. On high alert, he scanned for any clues he may have missed and watched for any signs of trouble. They arrived at a townhouse with a big patio. Monty noted the home overlooked the spot where Duchess had buried and lost her bone.

It was a warm evening. The front door was open. The party was in full swing, divided between the living room inside and the spacious patio outside. Many dogs were there, along with their humans. Monty heard music playing in the background. Sarah opened the patio gate. Monty strode through it. She followed, careful to close the gate behind her.

"Hello everyone!" Sarah called out.

Monty saw a pile of old bones on the patio. He wagged his stubby tail in appreciation. Sarah noticed them too. She stopped in her tracks.

"What's with all the bones?" she said.

This sparked laughter from the human party guests.

"We've been talking about that all evening," someone said.

"Yeah, the dogs are acting weirder than usual today!" said another.

The Party

Monty could have explained it to them, but he didn't bother. He knew none of the humans would understand. The dogs had done what Monty asked. Each brought a bone to the party and left it on a pile in plain sight. The placement could not have been more perfect: outside on the patio next to where the thief had dug up Duchess's choice bone.

All Monty had to do was get the dogs and people inside long enough for the thief to think it would be safe to raid this treasure trove.

Monty saw the Pug twins on the patio. They sat on the far side of the pile of bones, away from the gate. To his surprise, they both looked worried. After all their boasting about birthday parties, he expected them to be happy.

"Hey guys," Monty said. "What's the matter? Aren't you enjoying the party?"

"Hi Monty. No, nothing wrong," Licky said with a rather forced smile.

"Yeah. What did we tell you? It's awesome, right?" Sticky said. His smile didn't seem real either.

"Well, I only just got here," Monty said. "I haven't had time to check it out yet."

"Better get checking," Sticky said.

"Yeah," Licky added, "and make sure you wish a happy birthday to the guest of honor."

"The what?" Monty asked.

"Duchess. It's her birthday."

"You're supposed to wish her a happy one."

The Party

Monty gulped. He had hoped he could keep his distance from Duchess. But now it seemed he was expected to go right up to her, exchange sniffs, and be happy. Monty was certain Duchess would not be glad to see him. He started toward the townhouse door when one of the Pugs called after him.

"Monty?"

Monty turned around. Both Pugs once again looked nervous.

"We're gonna get that cat, aren't we?" Licky asked.

"Actually, it's not a cat," Monty explained. "It's a man pretending to be a cat. And I don't see how he could resist this prize."

That didn't seem to make them feel any better. When Monty turned to walk into the house, they followed as if they'd rather be anywhere than beside that pile of bones.

Monty stepped inside, eager to investigate. He had never been to this place before, and he had never been to a birthday party before. He was doubly curious to check everything out. He passed a box filled with ice. Inside were lots of bottles and cans stuck in the ice.

Dogs lounged on the floor, while their humans sat on the couch and chairs. The coffee table held packages covered in brightly colored paper. These must be Duchess's birthday presents. There were also drink glasses and a few more bottles, including one in a fancy velvet bag. Monty tried to puzzle out why

The Party

the humans kept some of their bottles on the table, and some in a box of ice on the floor. For that matter, why didn't they just drink the cool refreshing ice water? Throughout the home, there was a fabulous smell that could only be the cake. Wherever it was, Monty could not see.

Monty worked his way through the crowd of dogs. Most of them wanted to talk, which was fine with him. It stalled his inevitable face-to-face meeting with Duchess.

"What are we going to do when that cat burglar shows up?" said Zeek, a big, black, long-haired dog.

"It's not a cat. It's a —" Monty started to say until he was interrupted.

"Cat better not come near me, 'cause I'll bite him!" Sticky said.

"Yes, good," Monty said. "But it's a —"

"Cat burglar?!" Licky cut in. "More like cat burger if I catch him!"

Monty gave up correcting everyone that the burglar was not a cat. No one was listening. They would see soon enough. They all seemed afraid, even the ones that were bragging.

A small bark cut through the chatter, "That cat burglar took on Fritz!"

The dogs looked around. The bark came from Mildred, a puffy Pomeranian sitting on her human's lap.

Mildred continued, "Not one of you would dare enter the lair of Fritz the Ninja Cat, but this thief did, and he lived to tell the tale. I don't know how tough he is, but I sure don't want to find out!"

"That may be true. The man burglar," Monty said, stressing the word man, "may be tougher than any one of us. But he's no match for all of us. If we stick together, we will be fine. Now if you'll excuse me, I need to wish Duchess a happy birthday."

The dogs nodded their heads in agreement. Monty didn't really want to find Duchess. He wanted to be free of this conversation. Yet the dogs wandered off, and Monty had a clear path directly to Duchess.

Montgomery Schnauzer P.I.

The Party

She was at the far end of the room, lounging on her dog bed. The bed stood off the floor on stubby legs. The overstuffed pillow was ruby red. Sitting like that, elevated above the rest of the dogs, Duchess looked like royalty. She glared at Monty as if daring him to approach.

Monty stood frozen. He knew he should say something, but had trouble working up the nerve. Suddenly, Duchess stood up.

"You rotten weasel!" she said.

"Now now, Duchess, I know you're upset... But I have a plan and – "

She ran right past him.

Chapter Sixteen

Picking Bones

Monty followed Duchess as she ran outside. She barked angrily. Dogs scrambled out of her way. There on the patio stood Jiff, eyes wide with shock. He dropped a bone from his mouth. It landed at his feet with a thud. It looked delicious: a big beef bone with strands of meat clinging to the sides, and aged underground (judging by the clumps of dirt on it). It was just the kind of bone that dogs love.

"Lying, thieving, son of a cat!" Duchess said.

She collided with Jiff, knocking him back off his feet. He slid through the pile of bones, scattering them all over the patio.

She scuffed her feet, preparing a follow-up attack. Wendy stepped between the two dogs. Duchess tried to charge past her. Wendy grabbed Duchess by the collar and lifted the portly Bulldog's front paws off the ground. Jiff scrambled to his feet. He backed himself into a corner of the patio.

Duchess strained against her collar as she snarled at him, "It was you, you filthy mutt. You stole my bone!"

"I didn't, I swear!" Jiff said.

Duchess stopped growling. For a moment, she was calm. Monty grew suspicious. She

Picking Bones

was up to something; he just knew it. Wendy lowered Duchess to the ground.

"Wendy, don't do it!" Monty tried to warn her.

Wendy didn't understand, of course. When Duchess's feet touched the patio, she scooched backwards. Wendy's grip went slack, then her arm swung back behind her. Duchess jerked her head back. The wrinkles piled up on her thick neck and popped the collar right over her head. Suddenly free, Duchess tore around Wendy and renewed her attack. Jiff rolled on to his back to indicate submission.

Duchess pounced on him anyway. He squealed. She snapped at him between barking out insults.

"You soap-stinker! You're a thief! A crook! A mangy mutt!"

Montgomery Schnauzer P.I.

Picking Bones

She really did have the worst potty mouth Monty had ever heard.

Wendy reached in to try to separate the two dogs. Jiff wriggled to avoid Duchess's attacks. She snapped and snapped at him, almost biting Wendy. Wendy pulled her hands back. By then a crowd of dogs and humans had gathered around. A man arrived and pushed his way through.

"Duchess! Bad dog! What's the matter with you?!" he yelled.

He grabbed Duchess by the scruff of the neck and pulled her off Jiff.

Duchess spat one last curse, "I hope you get a bath!"

All the dogs gasped in shock. She had uttered the worst insult one dog can say to another! Jiff stared, slack jawed. Even Duchess sensed that she had gone too far. She went still and silent.

Wendy went to Jiff and made him sit. The man did the same to Duchess. Monty figured he must be Duchess's poppa. They held their dogs in place and talked to them in soothing but firm tones. Monty could tell this was unnecessary. The fight was over.

Monty doubted Jiff had stolen Duchess's bone. It didn't fit with the other details of this case: the bag of rocks, the high-rise burglaries, the man who fought Fritz. Monty knew they were connected to this bone somehow. He just couldn't prove it yet. He felt he ought to do something to help poor Jiff.

Monty walked into the middle of the crowd. The dogs parted to let him pass. He stopped between Jiff and Duchess. In situations like this, Sherlock Holmes would give a great and thoroughly convincing speech. Monty thought he should give that a try.

"My friends," Monty started, "Duchess..."

His voice failed. He was nervous. All eyes were on him.

"Jiff... did... did not steal your bone," he stammered.

He tried to summon the courage to continue. How did the great detectives do this? In all those classic books, they fought ruthless villains and grave injustices, but never did any of them wrestle with a fear of public speaking.

"I know this for a fact," he said.

And then he realized something. So many of those books used the phrase, "The facts speak for themselves." Monty never understood that (surely facts didn't speak), but now he did. If he stuck to the facts, he would know exactly what to say, and he did not need to be afraid.

"Facts!" he said and paused for effect. "They talk... see? And I'm going to tell you what they say."

That did not come out right, he thought. He scanned the surrounding faces to gauge their reactions. Duchess still looked put out. Oh well; Monty knew she would be the hardest to convince. The other dogs stared with their ears forward, eyes wide, and heads tilted to the side. Clearly they wanted to hear what he had to say. Monty's eyes settled on Jiff. The poor fellow looked worried.

"It will be OK," Monty whispered to him.

Monty turned to address his audience, "Fact number one: our friend Jiff is hardly the criminal mastermind type. No offense, Jiff."

"None taken," Jiff said.

"Humph!" went Duchess. "He could have found my hiding spot by accident and decided to help himself."

Monty responded, "This crime scene was more complicated than that. The thief brought the bag of rocks with him, dug up your bone, and planted the rocks in its place. And he went on to commit other crimes. Fact number two: the real burglar struck Jiff's home not one week ago, and was injured by Fritz the Ninja Cat."

"Jiff wouldn't rob his own house," Zeek said.

"I wasn't even there!" said Jiff. "I was at Grandma's."

"Right," Monty said, moving the conversation along before Jiff could launch into another Grandma speech. "Fact number three: the very next day, I saw a man come into the human hospital with injuries from a cat attack. I would have caught him too, if it wasn't for my stupid leash. But I got close enough to smell the cat hair on him. It came from Fritz. This was the man who tried to rob Jiff's house. That's right. The cat burglar is, in fact, a man."

Picking Bones

This sparked another gasp from the crowd of dogs.

Monty continued, "He acts like a cat to throw the police off the trail. It's working too. Last I heard, the police were still searching for a cat burglar."

"Finally, I believe I know how this bone came into Jiff's possession. He found it in his home the day after the burglary. Isn't that right, Jiff?"

"Yes, that's exactly right!" Jiff said. "How did you know?"

"If you found it, as you say, not in Duchess's hiding hole in the park, then you found it after the thief took it. We have to ask, when did your two paths cross? We know the man invaded your home. He must have had the

Picking Bones

bone with him. When Fritz attacked him, he must have dropped it in his haste to escape. It makes sense."

A murmur went through the crowd. Dogs nodded their heads and muttered to each other. Even Duchess was convinced. She sidled over to Jiff and gave him an apologetic sniff.

"I'm sorry, Jiff," she said.

"It's OK," Jiff said.

"I believe this belongs to you," said Monty, and he nudged the sumptuous bone over to her feet.

"Thanks," she said. "You really are a good detective."

Montgomery Schnauzer P.I.

She scooped up the bone. Carrying it in her mouth, she waddled happily inside to rejoin her birthday party.

Chapter Seventeen

The Scene of the Crime

At long last, the time came for cake. A human voice (Monty thought it belonged to Duchess's momma) called the guests into the house.

"Cake time!" barked Licky.

"Woo-hoo!" howled Sticky.

Both Pugs ran inside. The rest of the dogs stampeded after them. Monty waited outside. He wasn't ready to go in yet. Something still

Montgomery Schnauzer P.I.

bothered him about this case. Jiff stopped to talk to him.

"Thanks for sticking up for me, Monty," he said.

"That's what friends do, right? Besides, a detective always seeks the truth."

"Well, you're awesome at it. You solved the case. That must feel good."

That's the problem, Monty thought; it doesn't. He accomplished what his client had asked him to do. His job was done. He should go inside and celebrate with a big slice of doggy birthday cake. Yet he did not feel satisfied. Much like the twist midway through the story *The Big Sleep*, the case was over, but there was still an unanswered mystery.

The Scene of the Crime

Monty said, "No, I haven't solved it yet."

"What do you mean? Duchess got her bone back. You proved I didn't take it."

"That wasn't proof. It was a theory."

Jiff's expression changed. He looked hurt.

Monty continued, "I believe you didn't do it, Jiff. And I managed to convince the other dogs. But it won't be enough to convince a judge and jury. We need real proof."

Jiff tilted his head and asked, "Well how do we get it?"

Monty looked at the bones scattered around the patio. It was the largest collection he'd ever seen. And it had a purpose: to trap a thief. The party guests were all inside. There would never be a better time for Monty to see his plan through.

"We need to catch the real criminal," he said. "Help me gather these bones."

Monty picked up a bone in his mouth, carried it to the center of the patio, and dropped it. Jiff did the same. Together, they rebuilt the pile of bones. When they'd finished, Monty turned to face Jiff.

He said, "Now we hide and wait. I will stand over here and watch for the man burglar to come. You wait inside the door. When I give the signal, gather all the dogs to come help catch him!"

Jiff gave Monty an earnest nod, then trotted inside.

The Scene of the Crime

Monty waited.

He gazed out at the dog park. It was empty. The dogs and people that gathered there most evenings were all here at the party. The shadows of the trees grew longer. The sun was about to set.

Then his keen hearing picked up something moving in the park. He cocked his ears as far forward as they'd go, focusing on the sound. It sounded like digging. Someone was digging in the park. Monty stood on his hind legs to reach the townhouse window. He looked inside and counted the party guests. No one was missing. The humans chatted and sipped their drinks. The dogs waited for cake.

Montgomery Schnauzer P.I.

Monty crept to the patio gate, careful that his paws didn't make any sound on the concrete tiles. The pads on his paws were soft like the rubber shoes the storybook detectives often wore. Monty's master said they wore those shoes so they could sneak around without making noise. That's why the old stories called detectives "gumshoes."

Monty peered into the shadowy park. He saw a figure, all in black, digging at the spot where Duchess had lost her bone. Now that's puzzling, Monty thought. Why would the thief be looking there? He'd already stolen the bone from that spot. And if it was a bone he wanted, there was a big pile of them up on the patio. Why didn't he take the bait? What the bark was he looking for?

The Scene of the Crime

Then it occurred to him: the rocks!

There were two things in that hole. The thief knew where the bone went. That left the rocks. Monty wanted to howl. If only the police hadn't taken them away!

He tried to calm down. He needed to think. He didn't have the rocks, but maybe he didn't need them. He only needed the burglar to think he had the rocks. He needed a decoy. And he needed it fast. The burglar would soon find out that the rocks were no longer there.

Monty went into the townhouse. Jiff stood stiff as a board inside the doorway. It pleased Monty that his friend took his watch duty so seriously. The rest of the dogs had gathered in a circle. They stared up at Duchess's momma,

The Scene of the Crime

as she held the birthday cake on a tray. It smelled sweet and scrumptious.

Jiff said, "Hi Monty! I'm waiting for your signal, just like you told me..." Then he paused as his brain worked out why Monty had shown up inside. "Oh, you're here! The signal! It's time. I'll round up the dogs, just like –"

Monty grabbed Jiff by the tail to stop him from alerting the other dogs.

"Not yet," he said. "It's too soon. There's a snag in the plan. I don't have time to explain. I need you to help me make a bag of rocks."

"Alright!" Jiff said. "Um... how do we do that?"

"First, I need that fancy bag off the bottle that's on the coffee table. But when I try to grab it, the humans will see me. One of them will stop me for sure. I need a distraction."

Jiff thought for a moment then said, "I could pee on the inside rug. That always causes a huge scene."

"No, Jiff, no! That would make you a... make you a..."

"A what?"

Monty whispered, "A bad dog."

Jiff cowered a little. He only talked about doing a bad thing, and yet he still felt ashamed.

"Besides," Monty said, "the humans would banish you to outside – maybe all of us. And that would alert the burglar. No, it's a bold plan, but it will not work. We need something better."

The Scene of the Crime

"Okay everyone!" Duchess's momma's voice rang out over the crowd, "time to sing!"

She started singing *Happy Birthday*. Most of the guests joined in. Monty recognized at least one voice mumbling something different than the song.

Sarah said, "This is ridiculous."

No, Monty thought, it's pretty convenient! The guests focused their attention on Duchess or each other. Some sang. Some faked it. Some looked embarrassed. Some sang with far too much enthusiasm. But none of them paid attention to the coffee table. Monty made his move for the bottle. He grabbed the velvety bag in his teeth and pulled. The bottle slid off the table. It landed on the carpet with a soft thunk that only Monty heard. He slid the bag off the bottle and slunk away to hide behind the box of ice.

Monty looked around for Jiff and saw that his friend had joined the singing.

"To youuuuu-ah-woooo-oooo!" Jiff howled with the last notes of the song.

The humans burst out laughing. The dogs nodded in approval: "Very nice, very nice indeed."

"Pssst! Jiff, over here," Monty said.

Jiff rejoined Monty. He said, "Wasn't the singing wonderful?"

"That it was," Monty said. "Now we need to finish this. I need some little rocks to put in this bag."

The Scene of the Crime

"Right! I'm on it," Jiff said. He marched toward the outside door.

"No!" Monty said, and he grabbed Jiff by the tail again. "The burglar is out there. He will see you. We need to find some rocks in here."

"Um... well... what did the rocks look like?"

"They were small and clear and they kind of sparkled in the light."

"Like these cold rocks here in this box?"

Monty looked inside the box of ice. The ice chunks did look a bit like the rocks that were in the original bag. They were larger, but if he only put a few in the bag, it should look the same from the outside. If the burglar got close enough to tell the difference, Monty would be able to nab him.

"Good thinking," Monty said. "Help me put a little ice in this bag."

Jiff felt pleasantly surprised. He didn't get many compliments on his thinking skills. Monty picked up the bag with his front teeth and held it open for Jiff.

"Try to get small ones," he added.

Jiff scooped small chunks of ice in his mouth and dropped them into the bag. When Monty guessed they had enough, he signaled Jiff to stop. Jiff looked weird. His nose wrinkled up, and his eyes crossed.

"What's wrong?" Monty asked.

"C-c-cold," Jiff said. "Headache!"

"Oops, sorry! It will pass. Can you hold this for me so I can have a look?"

The Scene of the Crime

Jiff nodded, eyes still crossed. Monty passed the bag to Jiff. Then he stepped back to check their work. It looked pretty good. Monty wagged his stubby tail to show his approval. He nodded to Jiff, and the bigger dog passed the bag back.

"This is it, Jiff! I need you to watch and listen. When I bark up at you, I want you to gather all the dogs. OK?"

"Sure. Where are you going?"

"I'm going to catch the thief."

With the bag in his mouth, Monty snuck outside to the patio. He paused at the gate to open the latch using the trick Little Houdini had taught him. If he ever saw that pint-sized dog again, he would be sure to thank him. Monty left the gate open and went down the steps.

Montgomery Schnauzer P.I.

The Scene of the Crime

Moving as quietly as any gumshoe detective, he made his way to the scene of the crime.

The man had stopped digging. He stared into the hole. He stood up, scratched his head, and muttered to himself. He looked around, scanning the ground near the hole.

That was close, Monty thought. He leaned back, pretending to sit but ready to run at a moment's notice.

He barked, "Looking for these?"

Montgomery Schnauzer P.I. ─────────────

Chapter Eighteen

Face to Face

At the sound of Monty's bark, the man in black spun around.

"Hey! Uh... little fella," the burglar said. "Give me those."

He stepped forward. Monty sprinted away. That's it, Monty thought, come and get me! The thief stopped. Monty stopped. He turned around to see the man leaning forward with his hand out.

"Easy boy," the man said in a hushed pleasant tone, "Come here. I have treats."

Monty's ears pricked up. He liked treats. Even untrained street dogs knew that word meant free food. But he was not that easily swayed. He had a job to do.

Monty said, "No. You come here."

Then he trotted a few steps away and cast a look over his shoulder. He waited for the burglar to chase him. But the man stayed put. He put his hand in his pocket, fumbled around a bit, and held it out again.

"Come on," the thief said. "Here's a nice treat. Be a good doggy."

Monty found this oddly insulting. Normally he liked being called a good doggy. But this guy was a thief, an impostor dressed up as a cat, and an all-around bad guy! The last thing Monty wanted to be was this man's "good doggy."

"Not a chance, cat-man," he barked. "Come get your diamo-thingies."

The man did not budge.

Monty felt a cold drip on his paw. The ice was melting! The bag was wet already, and it would only get worse. Pretty soon there would be nothing left. He felt frustrated. He needed the burglar to chase him – now! He decided to take a risk. He crept closer.

"That's it. Come here," the man said, and he reached his hand out as far as it would go.

The thief held out a treat: a small brown square, moist and meaty. Monty was close enough to smell it, and it smelled heavenly. He regretted that he didn't get some of that birthday cake. He was hungry, and that treat was so tempting. His tummy rumbled. His

Montgomery Schnauzer P.I.

mouth watered. Drool dripped from his jowls. He could have that treat. All he had to do was open his mouth and take it.

"It's super-yummy. It's all yours. Just bring me the bag," said the man.

Wait, Monty thought. If he opened his mouth to get the treat, he would drop the bag. That would ruin his plan. The man was trying to trick him.

"No," Monty said, pulling his nose back. He felt a sense of smug satisfaction. Any ordinary dog would take the treat, but Monty chose to stay true to his purpose. He would not let a simple pleasure like a dog treat override his detective's duty.

Then Monty realized something. It was no accident that the man/cat burglar dropped

Duchess's bone at Jiff's house. He had brought it with him deliberately. He had found it in the park while hiding loot from a previous crime. He knew it would keep a dog busy for a long time — long enough to rob a home. So he had kept it, and he brought it with him to his next crime. He had intended to bribe Jiff the same way he was trying to bribe Monty now. So this was how he got away with his crimes. He used bones and treats to keep the dogs busy so that he could steal their humans' things.

"You make me sick, mister," Monty growled. He knew the man couldn't understand him, but he was too angry to care. He was going to tell this thief exactly what he thought of him. Monty took two steps back and plopped the bag down in front of him.

"You're a bad human!" he shouted.

"Easy boy... Quiet now... Shhh," the burglar said.

"What's the matter? Don't want to draw attention to yourself?"

The thief looked around nervously, trying to decide what to do. Monty worried he might run away. The burglar lunged forward.

"Give me those!" he shouted.

Monty scooped up the bag as quick as he could. The man fell on the grass, his hands landing where the bag used to be.

"Too slow, weirdo cat guy!" Monty said.

"Why you miserable mutt!"

The insult made Monty happy. The man was angry and frustrated — exactly what Monty wanted. He trotted away, fairly certain the foolish man would follow. He glanced back. Sure enough, the man climbed to his feet and ran toward him.

Monty ran off at a gallop.

Chapter Nineteen
The Chase

Monty ran with the burglar in hot pursuit. He swung back toward Duchess's townhouse. He saw Jiff standing watch on the patio. He may have issues, Monty thought, but he's trustworthy in a pinch. It was time to give him the signal.

Monty leapt in the air and shouted, "Hey Jiff! Call out the dogs!"

"Cat *bur-ger*!" Jiff barked, and he ran around the patio in circles shouting, "Cat! Cat! Cat!"

Licky and Sticky burst onto the patio.

"What is it?" One of them said. Monty was too far away to tell which one.

"Cat! Cat!" Jiff barked.

The Pugs looked around, then fixed their gazes into the park. They shot through the open gate and bounded down the stairs. Jiff followed. More dogs streamed out of the house. Some of them had trouble trying to squeeze through the gate all at once. Monty passed the townhouse. He couldn't see them any longer, but he could hear barking behind him. It sure sounded like a lot of dogs!

"Cat! Cat!"

"We're gonna get you, cat!"

"It's a man."

"Whatever!"

The Chase

"We're going to get youuu ah-wooo woo woo woof!"

Monty ran at a good clip, but not his top speed. Most dogs can run faster than most people. He didn't want to outrun the burglar. He wanted the man to keep chasing. He cast a glance over his shoulder to make sure the burglar wasn't too far behind. But the burglar was close — too close!

This man could run quickly. He was more like a cat than Monty thought. He also had a huge pack of dogs behind him, snapping at his heels. It looked like every dog at the party had joined the chase — even Mildred. The thief had to run fast, or the dogs would overwhelm him. Monty shuddered to think what they might do to the man.

Montgomery Schnauzer P.I.

The Chase

Monty sped up. They were locked in this chase now. This had to end without the man getting ripped into a thousand pieces by the dogs! Monty had to find someone to arrest him.

They left the park and sprinted down the sidewalk that ran between the ocean and the apartment buildings. Monty ran toward the coffee shop with one thought repeating through his mind: please be there, please be there, please be there!

He rounded the last corner with anticipation. He hoped to see the black police car, parked where the officers left it when they went on their breaks. It wasn't there. Oh no! Monty did not know what to do. Where should he lead the man next?

The Chase

He ran toward the police station, knowing in his heart that this was a bad move. The burglar was no idiot. He wouldn't be dumb enough to run right into the police station. Still, Monty had to keep moving while he thought of a better plan.

Monty rounded another corner. Up ahead he saw bright flashing lights on a big black car. The police officers had pulled someone over. Standing on the sidewalk next to the car was a familiar, tall, stately dog. After his humiliating arrest, Monty would recognize Constable Casey from any distance. This time, however, he was happy to see her.

He looked back over his shoulder. The burglar saw the police car and stopped abruptly. The swarm of dogs surrounded him, snapping and snarling. Yikes! Monty thought, the dogs have him trapped. He needed help desperately. Monty pushed himself to run faster.

"CASEY!" Monty shouted, above the din of barking dogs.

Casey turned around. Her keen ears pricked up. She strode forward as far as her leash would allow. The lady police officer holding the leash also turned around.

"Casey! I need your help!" Monty pleaded.

"You're off-leash again," Casey said.

"Never mind that! Don't you see what's going on down there?"

"I see," said Casey, calmly. "Leave that to the professionals. Everything must be done according to proper police protocol."

The Chase

Monty felt a flush of rage. She was so frustrating! Why did he think she would be reasonable?

"Greg," the police woman called to her partner. "You'd better wrap that up."

The other officer stepped away from the car, and looked down the street. He saw the large pack of barking dogs and the man all dressed in black dancing around to avoid them. He looked down at Monty, the small, cute dog with a blue satchel in his mouth. Then Greg looked back at the man in black.

"Is that – ?" Greg started to say.

"The jewel thief suspect?" the lady officer finished his sentence. "I think so."

Montgomery Schnauzer P.I. ─────────────

Officer Greg walked back to the car. Monty's gazed shifted back to the burglar. The man stood still now, surrounded by growling, nervous dogs. He stuck his hands in his pockets. Monty looked at the police. He thought, what's taking them so long?

Officer Greg spoke to the driver of the other car, "Today is your lucky day. I'm letting you off with a warning."

Monty looked at the burglar again. The sight made Monty drop the bag from his mouth. The man turned his pockets inside out, scattering a mess of treats all over the ground.

"Noooooo!" Monty howled.

The dogs dove for the scattered goodies, forgetting all about the chase. This gave the man the distraction he needed to slip

The Chase

away. The burglar ducked into an alley and disappeared from sight.

Ignoring the police, Monty turned back and sprinted after the burglar.

Montgomery Schnauzer P.I. ─────────────

Chapter Twenty

Dead End

Monty ran to the last place he'd seen the burglar. He darted around the corner and into the alley. It was darker than the street, yet he could still make out the features of the place. A dog's eyes are well-suited for low light. The alley extended away from the street and came to a dead end. A couple of big garbage bins crowded the space at the far wall. There were a few doors, most certainly locked. Next to one of these doors sat a big wooden crate with two plastic chairs beside it. Monty assumed someone used this as a table.

The man stood at the far end of the alley. His black clothing made him almost invisible in the shadows. He looked frantically from side to side. He had nowhere to go. Monty had him trapped! Behind Monty, the police were finishing up their business — their confounded protocol! All Monty had to do was keep the thief here until they arrived.

The burglar fixed his gaze on the wall behind the crate. There a pipe ran up the side of the building. Monty hadn't paid it any attention. To him it was simply part of the wall. It didn't seem important.

Well, it was very important to the cat burglar. He strode over to it, jumped up, and grabbed it. Then he started climbing.

"No!" Monty howled.

He sprinted forward, desperate to get to the thief before he climbed out of reach. As he closed the distance, he could tell the thief would win this race. Monty eyed the crate. If he jumped from there, he could reach the man. Monty veered to the nearest patio chair. He jumped up. He slid on the plastic, and the chair tipped. He jumped again. He got his front paws on the crate. His back legs slammed against its side. He scrambled up, thankful that the crate was made of wood, so he could dig his claws in.

From the top, he judged the distance to the climbing burglar. Monty thought he could make the jump, but it was risky. If he didn't grab onto the man, he would have a nasty fall to the pavement, and the criminal would escape yet again.

Montgomery Schnauzer P.I.

Monty ran and leapt. He hung in the air for a second. He then collided with the burglar's back, but he had nothing to hold on to. He slid a short way, biting the air as he fell. His jaws clamped on something firm. It smelled of leather. The sudden stop jarred Monty's teeth. Ouch, that hurt! He almost let go. But he was determined to keep the thief here. He hung on.

"Ow!" the man shouted. "Stupid dog!"

Monty hung by his teeth from the burglar's belt. He gripped it tight and tried to shake the man loose from the pipe. He kicked against the man's legs. He whipped his head from side to side. The man slid down. Monty's heart skipped. They were falling!

Dead End

The man caught his grip. They stopped falling, which jarred Monty's teeth again. Once more he fought the urge to let go.

The burglar tried to knock him off. The man wiggled his butt from side to side. The motion made Monty dizzy. His jaws ached. Still he hung on.

The man reached down with one hand, grabbed Monty by the collar, and pulled up. Monty felt his collar choking him. He clenched his jaws, determined to keep his grip on the man's belt. They slipped down a little more. The burglar braced his feet against the wall. Monty's chest bounced off the man's butt.

With a sudden crack, the pipe broke. They fell.

Dead End

Back out on the sidewalk, Jiff suffered a crisis of indecision. He wanted to help his new best friend, but the bad guy had dropped his favorite treats. He even knew the human name for them: *Droolies*. There were other treats as well, including a few strips of bacon and a small bone. But Jiff loved Droolies best of all. He couldn't decide: eat the treats or help his friend.

The other dogs had no such dilemma. They dove at the treats, barking and shoving each other. Jiff found himself crowded out. He couldn't see the treats anymore. He took too long to make up his mind, and the circumstances made the decision for him.

He left the other dogs and went looking for his friend.

Monty and the man toppled to the ground with a rough thud. Monty scrambled to get on his feet, but something held him back. The burglar still had a grip on his collar. The man held the broken length of pipe in his other hand. He used it as a crutch to climb to his feet.

Monty hung helpless in the man's grasp. His collar choked him. He couldn't bark for help. In fact, he found it hard to breathe. The world looked blurry through his eyes.

He saw a brown shape creep up the alley. The other dog's ears drooped backward and its tail curled between its legs. It was clearly frightened, and yet it advanced slowly.

"Jiff —" Monty tried to speak but could say no more. He wanted to warn his friend to stay away. The burglar was too dangerous. They had lost this fight.

"Now you're going to get it, you miserable meddling mutt!" the burglar said, and he held the pipe high over Monty's head. He lined up to strike.

Monty closed his eyes. His body tensed. He felt terrified for his life.

"Stop!" Jiff barked.

Monty opened his eyes. The brown shape of Jiff trembled in fear, yet he still snarled at the burglar.

"You heard him," came another booming bark. "Freeze, criminal!"

Farther up the alley, a fuzzy black, tan and blue shape charged toward them. Monty blinked several times to clear his vision. He saw a stately German Shepherd in a blue police vest leap into the air.

Constable Casey connected with the burglar's chest. The man fell back, releasing Monty's collar. Monty tumbled to the pavement. A clang echoed as the pipe hit the ground.

Monty got up. Casey had the cat burglar pinned to the ground. She stood on his chest. The man lay on his back, arms and legs in every direction. He looked like a squashed bug. When he tried to sit up, Casey growled at him, menacingly.

"Don't move," she said. "You have the right to remain silent. You have the right to have another human come collect you. If you don't —"

"Police! Stay where you are!" came a shout from the far end of the alley.

The two police officers approached, focusing their full attention on the burglar.

The lady officer shouted, "You're under arrest! Do not move! Stay down with your hands out!"

Monty laughed. It was funny to hear a human using her bad-dog-voice on another human. Officer Greg bent down to put handcuffs on the man/cat burglar.

Casey walked over to Monty. She fixed him with her typical no-nonsense stare. What was it with her? he thought.

"What's so funny?" she said.

Suddenly embarrassed, Monty said, "Um... oh... nothing,"

Casey's expression softened, but only slightly.

"Pretty good work," she said, "for an amateur."

Monty smiled. That was as close to a compliment as he could expect from her.

Chapter Twenty-One

Police Protocol

Jiff wagged his tail and said, "You did it, Monty!"

"Yes," Monty said. "But tell me one thing. What happened to the other dogs? Why did they give up the chase?"

"That's two things," Jiff said.

"They're both the same thing."

"I'm sorry, Monty, I tried. But the man... he had Droolies."

"Droolies?" Monty questioned, not sure what that word meant.

"You know: Droolies," Jiff said, and then he broke into song, "*Soft and meaty. They're so cool. Treats so good, they make a dog drool!*"

"Yeah, I think I know them."

Monty watched the arrest with interest. It was nothing like the descriptions in the crime stories. For one thing, it took a lot longer. The human version of reading his rights went on and on and on. Then the two police officers took photographs of the scene and wrote in notebooks. Finally, they walked the burglar to their car and locked him inside. All this gave Monty time to calm down from the excitement of the chase and the terror of fighting for his life. He felt aches and pains all over his body.

Police Protocol

A crowd of people gathered in the meantime. Monty recognized them from Duchess's birthday party. They came looking for their dogs. Monty heard Wendy's voice.

"Sarah! I found them!" she yelled.

She grabbed Monty and Jiff by their collars.

"Bad dog, Jiff! Bad!" she said, and she yanked on his collar in an angry rush to clip the leash on him.

Jiff hung his head in shame.

Monty winked at him and said, "Don't believe her. You helped your friend catch a notorious criminal. I'd say that's pretty good."

Sarah appeared out of the crowd.

Police Protocol

"Montgomery P. Schnauzer, what have you done this time?" she said. This was the first time that Sarah had used his full legal name.

"I caught the bone thief, Momma!" Monty said, wagging his stubby tail with pride. He so looked forward to the comfort of Sarah's big soft bed.

She didn't understand a word he said. She clipped the leash on Monty's collar and scolded him.

Sarah said, "You've really outdone yourself, mister! Not only did you escape – again – you took all the dogs with you. And where do I find you? In the middle of a police incident!"

Wendy said, "I guess you're really going to give him back after this?"

Montgomery Schnauzer P.I.

Monty said, "What? But, I…"

Wendy didn't wait for an answer from Sarah. She kept talking, "Hear me out. We should find him a home instead. I would take him, but… you know… my cat –"

Sarah interrupted, "Relax. I'm not giving him up."

"You're not?" Monty said, relieved.

"You're not?" Wendy said, confused.

Sarah didn't get a chance to explain because Officer Greg came over and started talking to them.

He said, "We need your contact information, as witnesses."

"Of course," Sarah said.

Wendy nodded.

He held a notepad and pen in his hands. As each woman gave her name and phone number, he wrote in his pad. When he finished, he looked at Monty and smiled. His eyes followed the leash to Sarah's hand.

He said to her, "Your dog is quite the little hero."

"No, he's not. He's a bad dog who ran away from me."

"In my experience, dogs don't run away. They run toward. Something catches their attention: a mail carrier, a kid on a skateboard, a squirrel, and they follow it. My guess is your little guy didn't like the look of this character, all dressed in black, creeping around your building, so he gave chase."

"Um… thanks," Sarah said. "I wouldn't have thought of it like that."

Then Officer Greg moved on, collecting contact information from the others in the crowd.

Wendy whispered, "That cop is kinda cute. Don't you think?"

"Shut up!" Sarah said in a playful tone, as she nudged Wendy with her elbow.

"I'm just saying."

Sarah didn't say anything further. Wendy changed the subject back to Monty.

"So, you're really keeping him?"

"Yes," Sarah said. "We need each other. Obviously, I need to work on his behavior. Does your offer for training lessons still stand?"

"Of course!" Wendy said.

"Maybe not at your house," Sarah added. "You know... your cat."

Both women laughed.

Sarah gave Monty's leash a tug and said, "OK, Monty. Come home with Momma."

Monty thought, Oh boy! She said it. She really said it! She wanted to be his Momma! His heart swelled with pride.

He said, "Coming, Momma!"

Montgomery Schnauzer P.I. ───────────

As they walked off together, Monty wondered what adventures awaited them in the future. After all, he was a *bona fide* detective now. Surely, his next case was right around the corner.

The End.

Monty's adventures continue in Book 2:

**Montgomery Schnauzer P.I.
&
the Callous Car Thieves.**

About the Author

This is my Poppa. He's a good human. He wrote this whole book! Except I wrote this bit. He speaks some dog language and learns a little more each day. I hardly ever have to bark at him. I have a Momma too. We all live together in a big city beside an ocean. We hope these stories will inspire people to adopt pets from shelters and be kind to animals and to each other.

~ **by Spencer**

Visit the author at: TimothyForner.com

Made in the USA
Monee, IL
10 March 2022